Song of the Oktahutche

Alexander Posey, about 1900. From Minnie H. Posey, comp., *The Poems of Alexander Lawrence Posey* (Topeka: Crane, 1910).

Song of the Oktahutche
Alexander Posey

COLLECTED POEMS

Edited and with an introduction by
MATTHEW WYNN SIVILS

University of Nebraska Press
Lincoln & London

© 2008 by the Board of Regents of the
University of Nebraska
All rights reserved
Manufactured in the
United States of America

Library of Congress Cataloging-
in-Publication Data

Posey, Alexander Lawrence, 1873–1908.
Song of the Oktahutche :
collected poems / Alexander Posey ;
edited and with an introduction
by Matthew Wynn Sivils.
p. cm.
Includes bibliographical references (p.   )
ISBN 978-0-8032-1079-0 (cloth : alk. paper) —
ISBN 978-0-8032-2053-9 (pbk. : alk. paper)
I. Sivils, Matthew Wynn, 1971–   II. Title.
PS2649.P55S66 2008
811'.4—dc22
2008020382

Set in Minion by Bob Reitz.

Contents

List of Illustrations *xi*
Editorial Note *xiii*
Acknowledgments *xvii*
Introduction *xix*

POEMS

[Take my valentine and be] 1
The Warrior's Dream 2
[And old or new, can records find] 6
Death of the Poets 7
Red Man's Pledge of Peace [circa 1893] 8
Red Man's Pledge of Peace [circa 1898] 10
Red Man's Pledge of Peace [ledger version] 11
The Burial of the Alabama Prophet 12
Twilight [Eventide] 14
[Autumn days—bright days of gold] 16
Death of a Window Plant 17
O, Oblivion! 20
Ye Men of Dawes 21
[Did'st thou see the spectral blossoms fall?] 23
[Oh, those voices now we hear] 24
[Forsooth, thou art so versatile, O Bob!] 25
[To allot, or not to allot] 26
[For two long days the polar breeze] 27
[The picnic's coming] 28
[The whippowill has come] 29
[Those bursts of oratory—how they stir the soul!] 30
Wildcat Bill 31
There's a Tide 32
[In UNCLE SAM'S dominion] 33

Lowyna 34
The Indian's Past Olympic 35
Cuba Libre 40
Callie 41
Mother and Baby 42
Daisy 43
The Squatter's Fence 45
The Conquerors 46
Lines to Hall 47
To Our Baby, Laughing [To Baby Yahola] 49
The Two Clouds 50
The Rattler 51
June [Midsummer] 52
The Idle Breeze 53
My Fancy [Fancy] 54
Autumn 55
[Oh, to loiter where] [A Rhapsody] 56
To a Hummingbird 57
To the Century Plant 58
Verses Written at the Grave of McIntosh 59
To the Summer Cloud 61
To the Crow 62
To a Snowflake 63
Sea Shells 64
The Bluebird 65
Coyote 66
Distant Music 67
Distant Music [early draft] 68
Earth's Lilies and God's 70
Her Beauty 71
[I sing but fragments] 72
Ingersoll 73
Life's Mystery 74
A Picture 75
Sequoyah 76
To Wahilla Enhotulle (To the South Wind) 77

[Upon Love's sea, our barques shall sail] [Drifting Apart]   79
What My Soul Would Be   80
In the Winter Hills   81
The Open Sky   82
Sunset   83
The Legend of the Red Rose   84
My Pearl   85
Brook Song   86
Prairies of the West   87
To Yahola, on His First Birthday   88
To a Morning Warbler   89
Lowena   90
[The Poet's Song]   91
[We take no notice of]   92
[Nature's Blessings]   93
Twilight [July 7, 1898]   94
June [July 10, 1898]   95
The West Wind [Husse Lotka Enhotulle]   96
Morning   97
The Athlete and the Philosopher   98
Eyes of Blue and Brown   99
Flowers   100
Mount Shasta   101
The Dew and the Bird   102
The Deer   103
Be It My Lot   104
When Love Is Dead   105
To the Morning Glory   106
To an Over-Stylish Miss   107
[Farewell, frail leaf]   108
The Sunshine of Life   109
Gone   110
Kate and Lou   111
My Hermitage   112
What I Ask of Life   114
A Glimpse   115

The Boston Mountains   116
By the River's Brink   117
By the Shore of Life   118
Chinkings   119
A Common Failing   120
A Fable   121
Epigrams   122
God and the Flying Squirrel (A Creek Legend)   124
In Tulledega   125
In Vain   126
The Inexpressible Thought   127
July   128
The Man-Catcher   130
Meaningless   131
The Milky Way   132
Miser   133
A Vision of June [Narcissus—A Sonnet]   134
Narcissus—A Sonnet   135
Not Love Always   136
On Piney   137
Our Deeds [A Simile]   138
Pedantry   139
Say Something   140
September   141
A Thin Quilt's Warmth   142
Thoughts   143
To a Common Flower   144
To a Face Above the Surf   145
To a Winter Songster   146
To Hall   147
To Jim Parkinson   149
Trysting [Then and Now]   150
Tulledega   152
A Vision   154
What Profit   155
When Molly Blows the Dinner-Horn   156

The Arkansas River   157
Assured   158
Lovingly [The Call of the Wild]   159
Limbo [Esapahutche]   160
[Every moment I flow]   162
Memories (Inscribed to my poet friend George Riley Hall)   163
The Mocking Bird   164
Spring in Tulwa Thlocco   165
Where the Rivers Meet   166
Ode to Sequoyah   167
Nightfall [Twilight]   169
An Outcast   170
Pohalton Lake   171
Shelter   173
To a Daffodil   174
Happy Times for Me an' Sal   175
[What sea-maid's longings dwell] [To a Sea Shell]   177
The Decree   178
Song of the Oktahutche   179
To a Robin   181
Bob White   182
The Blue Jay   184
Moonlight [In the Moonlit Wood]   185
The Haunted Valley   186
On the Capture and Imprisonment of Crazy Snake   187
The Fall of the Redskin (With apologies to Edwin Markham)   188
Fus Harjo and Old Billy Hell   191
Saturday (To my friend Jim Cowin)   198
The Evening Star   200
On Hearing a Redbird Sing   201
She Was Obdurate   202
What a Snap   204
It's Too Hot   205
Alex Posey Is Responsible   206
A Freedman Rhyme   207
The Creek Fullblood (With apologies to Edwin Markham)   208

Arkansaw   210
Checotah   211
O'Blenness   212
Hotgun on the Death of Yadeka Harjo   213
Again   214
All the While [Let Men Dispute]   215
[By the cardinal led aright]   216
Come   217
The Flower of Tulledega   218
For Me   221
Frail Beauty   222
A Glimpse of Spring   223
The Homestead of Empire   224
[In that valley country lying east]   226
Irene   227
On a Marble Medallion of Dante   228
On the Hills of Dawn   229
On Viewing the Skull and Bones of a Wolf   230
Pity   231
A Reverie   232
The Rural Maid   233
'Tis Sweet   234
To My Wife   235
To the Indian Meadow Lark   236
A Valentine   237
A Vision of Rest   238
Whence?   239
[With him who lives a neighbor to the birds!]   240

Appendix: A Ledger of Poems   241
Bibliography   245

Illustrations

Frontispiece. Alexander Posey, about 1900
1. Wynema and Minnie Posey, 1910   *xx*
2. Original title page for the 1910 edition of Posey's poems   *xxii*

Editorial Note

This edition presents a complete, accurate, and accessible collection of Alexander Posey's poems, a collection that represents—as much as possible—his creative wishes. The vast majority of these 196 poems have been long out of print, with many last seeing publication in late nineteenth-century Indian Territory newspapers. Plus, until now approximately 50 of the poems included in this edition remained as unpublished manuscripts housed solely in archives. By presenting these unpublished works, and by including numerous corrected versions of poems previously available only in corrupted texts, this edition stands as the first to reclaim Posey's poetry from problematic former editions and from archival oblivion.

The final version of any poem published while Posey was still alive takes precedence over all other versions of it. For works available in manuscript form only, that manuscript version appears here. In rare cases where substantial textual variations exist (e.g., more than simply a stray comma or a minor change in letter spacing), this edition includes both versions, allowing a view of how Posey revised his writing over time.

For twelve poems all we have left are the versions presented in Minnie H. Posey's 1910 edition of her late husband's poetry. As these versions are the only ones available, they are included in this edition; however, these versions are included only as a last resort because the 1910 edition contains substantial errors and even a few changes made by Minnie herself. In the text the twelve poems originating from a corrupt edition are identified.

A number of the poems collected here lack dates of creation, so a variety of strategies were employed to place these texts within a rough chronological order. Posey published much of his poetry in Indian

Territory newspapers, many that are now either rare or lost. To our great benefit, Minnie Posey maintained a set of scrapbooks devoted to her husband's work though she rarely provided any information about either the source of the clipping or the date of publication.

In some cases the provenance of a newspaper clipping can be derived from its distinctive typeface. Also, it is sometimes possible to date a clipping from clues found in Posey's journals or based on hints provided by the content of the poem itself. The same goes for Posey's manuscripts, which also often lack dates of composition. Posey wrote many of his manuscripts on the letterheads of the various schools where he worked, and by making the assumption that he only wrote on those different types of letterhead while employed at those institutions, those poems can be placed within a rough chronology based upon Posey's known job history. It is an admittedly imprecise method of dating the poems, but in the absence of any other record it remains the best way. Despite these efforts, twenty-four poems found in this edition cannot be dated and are simply placed alphabetically at the end of the collection.

The texts have been annotated for the ease of the reader, and source notes and supplementary information that appear after each piece help explain historical, biographical, and other obscure references in the poems. As most people will not read this book from front to back, the endnotes are repeated when their referents occur in more than one text. Care has been taken to retain Posey's sometimes nonstandard sentence structure and other elements of his style, but the inclusion of distracting editorial apparatus such as "[sic]" has been kept to a minimum by the silent emendation of obvious spelling and printer's errors. Posey's use of dialect has not been altered, and these instances were left as self-evident rather than clutter the text with distracting editorial intrusions.

Posey left many of his poems untitled; these poems appear using their first lines as substitute titles placed in brackets. For the poems that Minnie Posey renamed after her husband's death, Posey's original titles (when known) are given first and then Minnie's title immediately following it, in brackets. For the few poems that share the same title, dates are provided in brackets, which allow the reader to differentiate these works.

Posey's writing deserves conscientious preservation and study. He wrote the largest body of American Indian poetry of his day, and during his lifetime his poetry helped him gain a national literary reputation well before the notoriety that followed the publication of his satirical Fus Fixico letters. For decades the versions of Posey's poetry most accessible to the public were also the least accurate. This edition brings the work of this important American Indian writer to a new generation of readers and scholars.

Acknowledgments

Of all those who helped me with this edition, I must first thank Daniel F. Littlefield Jr. who not only generously opened his research files to me and provided expert advice but who also gave me the initial idea for this book. While working at the American Native Press Archives on a project that would eventually become my first edition of Posey's work, *Chinnubbie and the Owl: Muscogee (Creek) Stories, Orations, and Oral Traditions* (University of Nebraska Press, 2005), Dan mentioned that Posey's poems were also in dire need of attention. I then realized I was working on just the first part of a much larger project.

My mentor, Jeffrey Walker, provided inspired guidance, and his suggestions did much to improve this edition's direction and content. Brad Bays, William Merrill Decker, and Linda Leavell each supplied enthusiastic support for this project and provided excellent critiques of early drafts.

I owe much to the librarians, archivists, and other staff members of the Gilcrease Museum in Tulsa, Oklahoma. In particular, I owe a great debt to the late Sarah Erwin, whose knowledge of, and care for, the Gilcrease's manuscript collection helped make this book—and several others—possible.

I also thank the librarians and archivists of the American Native Press Archives at the University of Arkansas at Little Rock; the Bacone College Library in Muskogee, Oklahoma (especially Francis Donalson); the Oklahoma Historical Society in Oklahoma City; and the University of Oklahoma's Western History Collection in Norman, Oklahoma.

Finally, for her unwavering support, I thank my wife—Alisa.

Introduction

Born on August 3, 1873, the Muscogee (Creek) writer Alexander Lawrence Posey lived most of his short life in the Muscogee (Creek) Nation in what is now part of the state of Oklahoma. During that short life he managed to become one of the most influential American Indian literary figures of his era.

One of Posey's dearest literary subjects was the Oktahutche, a river that meanders through the countryside and meanders through his poems. His entire life was tied to the Oktahutche and, as Daniel F. Littlefield Jr. writes, the young man, "had grown up near the river, swum in it, fished in it, written about it and taken float trips to observe the plants and animals along its banks."[1] Posey so loved this river that in his poem "Song of the Oktahutche" he gives the river a voice and allows it to speak. One stanza reads:

> O'er shoals of mossy rocks and mussel shells,
>   Blue over spacious beds of amber sand,
> By cliffs and coves and glens where Echo dwells—
>   Elusive spirit of the shadow-land—
> Forever blest and blessing, do I go,
> A wid'ning in the morning's roseate glow.

These words reveal the complex character of Posey's literary imagination. His poetry—drawing upon romantic, European, and Euro-American influences such as Robert Burns and John Greenleaf Whittier—becomes a sort of Indian Territory pastoral, a literary terrain in which Echo, the Greek nymph, shares a river with Stechupco, the "Tall Man" spirit of the Muscogees.

On May 27, 1908, Posey drowned while attempting to cross the Oktahutche, the very river he had praised in his poetry. In an obituary,

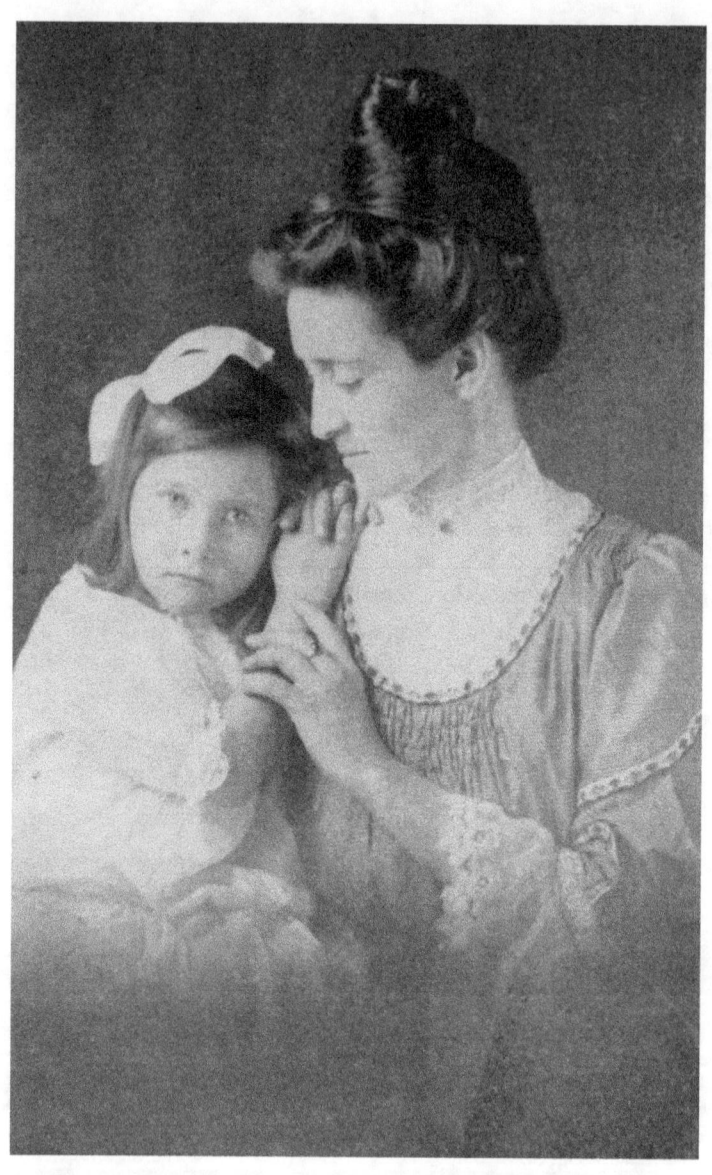

1. Wynema and Minnie Posey, 1910. From Minnie H. Posey, comp., *The Poems of Alexander Lawrence Posey* (Topeka: Crane, 1910).

Posey's friend and fellow Muscogee writer Charles Gibson hinted that the young poet's death may have been an act of punishment exacted by Muscogee spirits angered over his role in selling tribal land. Gibson writes, "He loved the old river that in a moment of rage extinguished his young life."[2] Contemporary Muscogees such as Craig S. Womack still affirm these sentiments: "Some say, Posey was drowned by Tie-Snake, swallowed up by the very river he loved, the Oktahutche."[3]

Twenty months after his death, Posey's wife, Minnie, worried that her husband's literary legacy had begun to fade. Most of his work—despite its popularity during his lifetime—remained either unpublished or lay yellowing in old issues of Indian Territory newspapers such as *Twin Territories* and the *Indian Journal*. Knowing that her husband's writing risked falling into obscurity, Minnie developed a plan to publish what he had left behind. First on her list was a book of poetry. She wrote that "the title of the book is, 'Song of the Oktahutche, and Other Poems'. . . . As soon as this book is out I will take steps to get the 'Fus Fixico' Letters, out. There is [sic] also many legends and stories—field notes & journals that would make an interesting volume."[4]

After selecting 105 of her husband's poems, works she thought "very pretty" (M. Posey to Barde, February 3, 1910), Minnie submitted the manuscript to three major publishers of the day: Houghton Mifflin, Scribners, and McClurg. She was able to court the best publishing houses because Alexander Posey had been more than just locally famous. At the height of his celebrity the reprints of his poems and satirical "Fus Fixico Letters"—along with articles about the talented Muscogee (Creek) writer and newspaper editor himself—appeared in such newspapers and magazines as the *Kansas City Star*, the *Criterion*, the *St. Louis Republic*, the *Kansas City Times*, the *New York Evening Sun*, the *Red Man*, the *Kansas City Journal*, *Indian's Friend*, the *New York Herald*, the *Philadelphia Press*, the *Boston Transcript*, the *New York Times*, as well as several other national publications (Littlefield 118, 183–85). Newspapers in such faraway locales as New York and Philadelphia asked Posey for regular contributions, and he was even invited to participate

2. Original title page for the 1910 edition of Posey's poems, *The Poems of Alexander Lawrence Posey* (Topeka: Crane, 1910).

in a lecture tour of American Indian figures (184). Still, each publisher rejected Minnie's manuscript.

Minnie blamed herself for this failure and bemoaned her lack of expertise in the matter: "I have had no assistance in preparing or collecting the poems and I feel so incompetent" (M. Posey to F. S. Barde, February 3, 1910). William E. Connelley, a former director of the Kansas State Historical Society, stepped forward to help her secure a publisher, and later that year the Topeka, Kansas, publisher Crane and Company released a handsome volume entitled *The Poems of Alexander Lawrence Posey*. The book included all the poems Minnie had originally selected along with a lengthy biographical essay penned by Connelley. Minnie's original title for the book had apparently fallen by the wayside, but she had at least accomplished her dream of publishing a book of her husband's poems. Posey's death had left Minnie in a bleak financial situation, and in addition to her motive of preserving her husband's writing she probably hoped to use the proceeds from the book to help provide for their two children, Yahola and Wynema.

Unfortunately, sales of the book were poor. "They were so bad," Daniel F. Littlefield Jr. writes, "that the publisher ultimately destroyed the stock of books and plates and returned the copyright to Minnie" (264). The disappointment was too much. She tabled her plans to publish her husband's other works and devoted herself to teaching at a variety of government-operated Indian schools and raising her children. Though no one wanted to publish a book-length version of Posey's work, unscrupulous archivists, newspapermen, and scholars repeatedly victimized Minnie, eventually absconding with both Posey's manuscripts and a collection of Muscogee artifacts (262–68).

While her intention to protect and promote her husband's poetry was admirable, Minnie also shares blame in corrupting Posey's published work, and her 1910 edition of his poetry actually did more harm than good to his literary reputation. In a letter bemoaning the trouble of finding a publisher who was willing to publish the poetry manuscript, Minnie betrays the nature of her collection: "Of course I have not attempted any changes or made any corrections. Mr. Posey was very modest & placed little value on any thing that he wrote. Many of the little verses that to me are very pretty—I am sure he would not have consented to their being included in a volume" (M. Posey to F. S. Barde, February 3, 1910). Thus, Minnie selected only those poems she liked—works she found "pretty"—and omitted scores of his other, often better, verse.

Even more damning was that, despite her claim that she had "not attempted any changes," she had indeed altered a few of her husband's poems. She sometimes selected older versions that he had since revised or introduced transcription errors, and in some cases even altered poems to her liking. Changes to Posey's manuscripts in Minnie's handwriting prove she sometimes supplied new titles, cut poems in two (e.g., dividing "Distant Music" into two "new" poems), and even rearranged stanzas within poems. Her reasons for these changes probably originate from an ill-conceived desire to improve the poems—at least in her opinion. Other changes may stem from her dislike of Posey's religious skepticism and may represent an urge to censor his questioning of organized religion, especially Christianity. Following Posey's death Minnie fought against accusations that her husband was an atheist, despite the strong evidence found in his eulogy of his Muscogee friend D. N. McIntosh and his open admiration of religious skeptics.[5] Minnie's wish to cover up her husband's ideas on religion may also explain why a large section of an earlier poetry ledger of Posey's is missing several of its pages. Perhaps those works disclosed beliefs she found unacceptable.

Early Poetry

Today the key to understanding Posey's beliefs and his writing can be found in how his traditional Muscogee upbringing merged with his exposure to an uncommonly advanced education for the typical Muscogee of his time. This unique amalgam of influences found its way into his poetry, and an examination of how Posey developed as a poet brings to light this complex melding and molding of influences and reveals a strong and often perplexing poetic voice.

The earliest of Posey's poems originate from his days as a student at Bacone Indian University in Muskogee, Creek Nation, where his education allowed him access to a library, a printing press, and supportive teachers. On June 11, 1890, at the end of his first year at Bacone, Posey's favorite teacher, Miss Anna Lewis, presented him with a copy of C. M. Kirtland's *Language and Poetry of Flowers*. (This book remains in Posey's personal library, held at what is today Bacone College in Muscogee, Oklahoma.) On page forty-eight (in the Narcissus section) there appears what is perhaps Posey's first extant poem, an early draft of his sonnet "Narcissus." Another early example of Posey's verse is an untitled valentine poem that begins with the line "Take my valentine and be" and ends with an unexpected punch line that proves Posey already had the makings of a humorist well before he began to write in earnest.

During his time at Bacone, Posey worked at both the library and on the university's newspaper, the *B.I.U. Instructor*. He had worked on a newspaper before, helping to edit the Eufaula *Indian Journal* (Littlefield 38), but his work on the *B.I.U. Instructor* seemed to coincide with his first experiments as a writer. Only one complete copy of this newspaper is extant, but thanks to Minnie, who kept a variety of undated clippings in her scrapbooks, we have early works that demonstrate he did more than just set type and write short articles for the paper. He submitted for publication several poems and short stories, at times even printing pamphlets of his work in the characteristic type of the *B.I.U. Instructor* press. It seems Posey instantly sought publication for his work and took great pains to present himself as a publishing writer from about 1892 on.

Posey signed his earliest poems as A. L. Posey but soon did something that would become common in his later work: he took on a thinly veiled pseudonym that also functioned as a literary persona. In about 1893 Posey began signing most of his writing (other than the Fus Fixico letters and his orations) with the name "Chinnubbie Harjo." At about this same time he wrote at least four short stories that related tales of a mischievous trickster figure of the same name. In claiming

Introduction xxv

this pseudonym Posey took the mask of a trickster poet, a persona he later refined as Fus Fixico. Poems such as "The Warrior's Dream," "Red Man's Pledge of Peace," "The Burial of the Alabama Prophet," and the long narrative poems "The Indian's Past Olympic" and "Fus Harjo and Old Billy Hell" all probably originate from this early period because Posey took scenes, traditions, and figures from his childhood and put them into a structured poetic form.

Yet even in these early days Posey's favorite poetic subject was the natural world. His early poem, "Twilight [Eventide]," which he published in pamphlet form, emphasizes a grandiose admiration for nature. He begins the poem with a type of verse that would become characteristic of much of his work:

> Beyond the far-off waves the seagulls cry,
>   As twilight shades
>   The emerald glades
> And zephyrs waft the strains of nightbirds nigh,

Posey's nature is one of grand implications, of the wind romanticized into "zephyrs" and of cow pastures molded into "emerald glades." He would remain an unapologetic dreamer for the whole of his short life, and this same romanticized worldview caused Posey to cultivate the persona of the genteel, well-read, and witty poet who was never too busy to stop to inspect a flower.

In 1894 the Dawes Commission began to makes its presence felt in Indian Territory, and Posey seems to have taken instant notice of the problems associated with the commission's goal of convincing the people of the Five Tribes to accept allotment and abandon their tribal government. Though always of a progressive bent, Posey distrusted the Dawes Commission and vented his feelings in the form of two poems, "O, Oblivion!" and "Ye Men of Dawes." These two works presaged his Fus Fixico letters as well as a number of later poems that took as their subjects political issues ranging from Eufuala's battle for county seat to Cuba's fight for independence from Spain.

By this time Posey had also started to serve as the Bacone Indian University correspondent for the Eufaula *Indian Journal*. He sent weekly notices of the goings-on around the college and often included short poems along with these tidbits of news. Most of these snippets display the author's love for the pastoral, but sometimes they take on a political stance, such as in his poem "[To allot, or not to allot]" in the March 1, 1894, issue of the *Indian Journal*. Posey's college education, love of reading, and political opinions had started to influence his poems, and he was not shy about publishing those opinions. He seemed to understand the power of the printed word from an early age. For example, as an accomplished orator Posey delivered four political speeches in the early 1890s but he was always careful to also present these orations in written form by publishing them in local newspapers or self-publishing them as pamphlets.

In the December 12, 1894, issue of the *Indian Journal* he published the poem "Wildcat Bill," which would be one of his first experiments in merging regional dialect and humor with social commentary. The poem parodies the type of European-American immigrants he saw in Indian Territory, a group of uneducated braggarts for whom he provides a comical voice. This kind of satire became one of Posey's trademark literary approaches, and it suited him well even at an early stage of his writing career. He ridicules the self-styled cowboys who had increasingly become an unwelcome presence in Indian Territory and does so in an intellectual manner that serves as a challenge to three commonly held racist views of the time: that education was wasted on American Indians, that Indians were incapable of creating meaningful art and literature, and that Indians were stoic and humorless. Posey's writing demonstrated that American Indians could express themselves intellectually and they had something to say about the latest chapter in a centuries-old series of abuses stemming from European-American imperialism.

Politics and Poetry

After 1895 Posey entered a transitional period in his life. He left college and briefly worked for the Brown Brothers mercantile company in Sasakwa, Seminole Nation. Never one to stay away from home for long, he spent approximately two months at the job before returning to Eufaula, where he entered Muscogee politics (Littlefield 70–71). Only two poems can be attributed to Posey for the year 1895, and even these are of uncertain authorship. The poems "There's a Tide" and "[In UNCLE SAM'S dominion]" (both published in the *Indian Journal*) are probably his handiwork, but while they bear the mark of his wit, they lack a signature.

In December of 1895 Posey's political contacts helped him secure a two-year appointment as superintendent of the Creek Orphan Asylum in Okmulgee (79). The job allowed him to hire others to manage a large portion of the day-to-day work, leaving him with an amount of free time he had not enjoyed since his boyhood. As he settled into life at the orphan asylum, which also served as a school, he took advantage of the opportunity to enjoy the companionship of Minnie and friends such as George Riley Hall. Only three poems can be dated to Posey's first year at the orphan asylum: "The Indian's Last Olympic," "Cuba Libra," and a manuscript of a love poem to his wife titled "Lowyna." However, "The Indian's Last Olympic," with its traditionally inspired treatment of the Muscogee Green Corn Ceremony and its signature line of "A. L. Posey," probably derives from his earlier Bacone work. "Lowyna" stands as the first of five love poems Posey wrote to his wife over his short lifetime; it is also the first time he uses his pet name for her in print (he later changed the spelling to "Lowena").

The development of Posey's political ideology becomes apparent in "Cuba Libra," a work of doggerel that champions the Cuban uprising against Spain and demonstrates how his political interests sometimes left the borders of Indian Territory. Despite its weaknesses, the poem does manage to present an interesting and empathetic voice, one from a fellow victim of colonial pressures and injustices. Posey's exclamation of "Down with tyranny!" arose from a man who belonged to a nation victimized by an unjust, imperialistic system.

Between 1897 and 1900 Posey's poetic output skyrocketed. While working in a series of administrative posts within the Muscogee Nation's education system he had the free time necessary to write approximately 130 poems. The majority of these poems are undated, but he usually drafted his work on the stationery of whichever educational post he then occupied. This tendency, coupled with a few clues derived from his journals, allows for a rough chronology of his poetic efforts. Throughout 1897, his last year as superintendent of the Creek Orphan Asylum, he wrote poems betraying a strong debt to the work of Percy Bysshe Shelley and other Romantic poets. While his earlier verse had created an idealized Indian Territory of "zephyrs" and "glades," he began to populate his vision of the natural world with figures from his reading, especially from Greek mythology, while also further introducing Muscogee figures and traditions. By merging the European-American traditions he read about in books with his own Muscogee culture, Posey creates an idealized poetic world that arose from his unique education and worldview. For instance, in "Lines to Hall," a poem in which Posey calls for his friend Hall to retire to the woods for poetic inspiration, he writes, "get thee to a hut/ Along some Tulledegan creek./ High life ill suits thy muse. Go put/ Her up an altar on the moor." Posey then ends the poem in the same vein when he asks Hall to relate the Muscogee oral tradition of the lost hunter:

> Tell how that Indian hunter died
> > That wintry day between the hill
> And frozen river; how he cried
> > In vain for help, and how he still
>
> Is heard on stormy nights to cry,
> > And beat the wolves without avail;
> And how his bones were left to dry
> > And scatter in that lonely vale.

This is an Indian Territory that could exist only in the mind of a Muscogee who had been educated at a Euro-American college and who was able to merge the images and ideas he admired from his

Introduction   xxix

prolific reading with comparable images from his own culture. His amalgamation of classical western mythology and Muscogee (Creek) tradition stands as one of his most remarkable, and least recognized, literary accomplishments.

In 1897 Posey began writing what would become a large body of poems devoted to birds, flowers, and sometimes other denizens of his unique literary Indian Territory. At moments he combined his love of dialect writing with his penchant for animal poems. "The Rattler," for example, presents the humorous vernacular of an unidentified man as he comments on an encounter with an overgrown rattlesnake: "If he were once to nip you on/ The thigh, you'd cross the Great Divide/ In just about as many steps!" While the poem itself appears unremarkable, the dialect of the narrator and the presence of a silent character whom the speaker addresses without reply both reveal how Posey experimented with voice. As with his later masterwork of dialect humor, the Fus Fixico letters, Posey's "The Rattler" offers a voice who is both funny and genuine—who is both the teller of and the butt of the joke.

Posey and Minnie's first child, Yahola, was born in March 29, 1897, and the new father took his son as the subject of one of his most touching poems, "To Our Baby, Laughing [To Baby Yahola]." In lines that would seem prescient a decade later, when Posey's early death left his children fatherless, he writes:

> If I were laid beneath
>   The grasses there,
> My face would haunt you for
>   A while—a day maybe—
> And then you would forget,
>   And not remember me.

His work is often at its best when dealing with his love of family and friends, and this poem, while sentimental, shows the range of Posey's poetic sensibilities. Capable of penning funny doggerel about a rattlesnake or, in this case, a serious poem commenting on his own mortality and eventual legacy, Posey did not shy away from a gamut of topics.

The Refusal of Fame

Through 1897 and 1899 Posey increased his poetry submissions to local newspapers and his work began to appear in print throughout the region. Printed in low numbers on paper with a high acid content in a territory ill-suited for archival collection, newspapers from this period are scarce. Sources held in the Gilcrease Museum in Tulsa, in the Oklahoma Historical Society in Oklahoma City, and in the American Native Press Archives in Little Rock, Arkansas, reveal that during the early days of Posey's most productive years, he published poems in the *Checotah Inquirer*, the *Muskogee Phoenix*, the Eufuala *Indian Journal*, and in the influential Indian Territory literary magazine *Twin Territories*. As his later enigmatic rejections of widespread literary popularity demonstrate, Posey sought publication on his terms for what he viewed as his own people of Indian Territory (Littlefield 118–19, 184–85).

If 1897 marked the sprouting of Posey's poetic output, the years of 1898 and 1899—when he worked as the superintendent of public instruction for the Muscogee Nation—represented its flowering. By 1899 he began to gain notice from readers outside of Indian Territory. National newspapers began to print and sometimes reprint his poems but, in a move that remains hard to understand, he refused to take advantage of this newly found fame. Though editors wrote him asking for poems, articles, and personal information, he shied away from the spotlight (118–19).

Yet he did seem interested in preserving his poetry. In a manner as enigmatic as he himself was, Posey handwrote a copy of about sixty-five of his poems into a self-contained bound ledger. Judging from the specific poems that were included, he probably compiled this handwritten collection between late 1898 and early 1899. The exact number of poems Posey entered into the ledger is unknown because several pages were removed and his reasons for creating this single handwritten collection remain unclear. Some poems remain unchanged but others, even some he had already published, display alterations. As Littlefield points out, Posey "either could not or did not intend to distinguish between his best and worst verse, for the collection contains both, ranging from his earliest to his most recent works" (120). The collection might have been the beginnings of a book of poetry, but as it is handwritten rather than typed, the intention seems of a more personal nature. Maybe he wished to give a handwritten copy of his favorite poems to his children or to Minnie, but there is no dedication, no hint at what he proposed to do with the strange gathering of poems. (The poems found in the ledger have been integrated into this edition with notes indicating their variants, and the appendix features the table of contents for the original ledger.)

By the end of 1900—the year that Posey's verse drew a large degree of national attention—he had all but ceased writing poetry. Only one poem can be dated to this period, "The Haunted Valley," which was written on Wetumka National School stationery. It would seem that the death of his infant son Pachina in 1900 had taken its toll on the young poet. Also, he may have realized that his poetry rarely met with his own high standards. The few poems that appeared in print between 1900 and 1902 were often holdovers from his earlier days of steady output. Though published in 1901 and 1902, the poems "The Fall of the Redskin," "Fus Harjo and Old Billy Hell," "Saturday," "The Evening Star," and "On Hearing a Redbird Sing" almost certainly date to earlier years. In fact, the longer narrative poem, "Fus Harjo and Old Billy Hell," may be a relic of his Bacone days that now is available only in the form of a later reprint. As with many of Posey's enigmatic decisions, few clues remain as to why he so abruptly ended his career as a poet.

In 1902 he began writing his satirical Fus Fixico letters, and these works became his main literary focus. He did continue to pen the occasional verse, but virtually all of the poetry he wrote in the last five years of his life took the form of editorial doggerel. These light poems variously condemn the unethical practices of the Dawes Commission

("It's Too Hot" and "The Creek Fullblood"), deride political figures ("It's Too Hot" and "Alex Posey is Responsible"), praise conservative Muscogees as "noble savages" ("The Creek Fullblood"), make racist comments against those of African heritage ("A Freedman Rhyme"), or attempt to foil the rival town of Checotah's chances at becoming the McIntosh county seat ("Checotah" and "O'Blenness"). The only notable poem from this period is "Hotgun on the Death of Yadeka Harjo," a work that mourns the death of a conservative Muscogee leader Posey respected. This poem, published in January of 1908, melded his earlier verse experiments with his masterful use of Muscogee full-blood dialect. The poem stands as both a reminder of the best of his earlier poetry and an example of the type of work he might have pursued had he not drowned crossing the Oktahutche River in May of that year.

Creation of an Indian Territory Pastoral

Posey wrote the largest body of American Indian poetry up to his time, and his poems represent a decisive cultural moment in American and American Indian literary history. In writing about the quality of his poetry, Littlefield argues that while much of Posey's work displays "sentimentality, halting lines, and weak endings," Posey at times also manages to reveal "striking, sometimes brilliant images" (105). All of his work succeeds in one central way: with these poems Alexander Posey gained something that had eluded almost every American Indian writer before him and too many after, that is, a national literary reputation as a serious writer.

As with his works in other genres, Posey's poems draw from a host of Euro-American influences that were, in turn, modified by his Muscogee heritage. In so doing he provides a gateway into a unique literary world found nowhere else. His work reflects his own vision of the Muscogee Nation and of Indian Territory as a whole, at a time in which these worlds were—through the dealings of the U.S. government—coming to an end. Posey then overlays his Euro-American influences onto what are often uniquely Muscogee images, cultural references, and humor.

It is unsurprising that he is at his best when he writes about his own culture, about the political injustices levied against his nation, about tribal members he respected, and about home.

Poems such as "Autumn," "To a Hummingbird," "Song of the Oktahutche," and "Tulledega," along with the heretofore unpublished "The Blue Bird" and "Callie," all stand as some of the best poetry by any poet from that period. Some poems are remarkable for a variety of reasons not directly related to sheer poetics. For example, Posey's political and humorous works—such as "Wildcat Bill," "Ye Men of Dawes," "[To allot, or not to allot]," "Cuba Libre," "The Fall of the Redskin," and "On the Capture and Imprisonment of Crazy Snake"—serve as fascinating accounts of contemporaneous Indian Territory political thought by a man who not only reflected the times but helped shape public opinion through newspaper editorials, orations, and his role as an educator.

Posey's cultural traditions and his copious reading habits led to a writer who drew from a deep well of resources. Not surprisingly, this diversity of influences led to him writing an equally diverse body of poetry that can best be understood when organized into four roughly delineated and sometimes overlapping categories of subject matter: an idealized natural world, Muscogee (Creek) cultural traditions, Indian Territory humor and wit, and personal works (i.e., poems devoted to family, friends, and sometimes even enemies). Almost all of his poems share at least a couple of these subjects and, as one might expect, his best works emerge when he finds inventive ways to combine multiple subjects within an individual poem.

At other times his poems become what Littlefield describes as "metrical experiments" in which "his free verse . . . was not always entirely 'free' but included unrhymed metrics in which he created an unusual effect with the unaccented end of one line and the accented beginning of the next. Other poems appear to be merely experiments in rhyme" (105–6) that take on the subject of a romanticized natural world far removed from its Indian Territory inspiration. "The Deer" serves as a good example of how Posey at times appears to marginalize his subject matter for exactly the metrical tinkering and rhyme experiments Littlefield describes:

> From out the folded hills,
>   That lie beneath a thin blue veil,
> There comes a deer to drink
>   From Limbo's waters in the dale.
>
> Then flies he back into
>   The hills, and sitting here, I dream
> And watch, as vain as he,
>   My image lying in the stream.

In this and many similar works, Posey echoes the influences of his favorite poets, often those who worked in the romantic and genteel traditions. Doubtless few of the people who lived near Limbo Creek in the Muscogee Nation envisioned the river as winding through a "dale." The stamp of Posey's readings in James Russell Lowell, Whittier, William Cullen Bryant, Henry Wadsworth Longfellow, Shelley, and many others marks these poems, but his reason to imitate their works stems from his task of finding language equal to the challenge of inscribing his own cherished Muscogee worldview into the English language.

In his tendency to choose diction that seems to clash with the subject matter, Posey emulates those Euro-American influences he thought most closely matched his own aesthetic sensibilities. After all, he did not speak or write in English until about the age of fourteen, and he chose the form and style of English (at least in terms of poetry) that he thought best reflected the way he viewed his natural environment. In an oft-quoted statement, Posey writes, "All of my people are poets, natural-born poets, gifted with wonderful imaginative power and the ability to express in sonorous, musical phrases their impressions of life and nature."[6] He continued by explaining his view of how Creek literature—in this case an oral literature contained within a viable indigenous language—is, at its heart, similar to the work of the romantic

Euro-American poets he admired. He argues that many songs, poems, and other works in the oral tradition "have a splendid dignity, gorgeous word-pictures, and reproduce with magic effect many phases of life in the forests—the glint of the fading sunshine falling on the leaves, the faint stirring of the wind, the whirring of insects."[7] Coming from Posey such a statement carries with it certain problems because he simultaneously champions his culture's richness and validity while also falling into the trap of romanticizing that very culture. Here Posey becomes susceptible to the "noble savage" stereotype, a portrait that sacrifices the humanity of American Indians for an unrealistic and nostalgic ideal that actually does more to reflect Euro-American anxieties than any American Indian reality. Further demonstrating his tendency to romanticize, Posey continues with the assertion that "the Indian talks in poetry; poetry is his vernacular—not necessarily the stilted poetry of books, but the free and untrammeled poetry of Nature, the poetry of the field, the sky, the river, the sun and the stars. In his own tongue it is not difficult for the Indian to compose,—he does it instinctively."[8]

His romanticized portrayals also creep into his poems dealing with individual American Indian figures, such as Chitto Harjo in the poem "On the Capture and Imprisonment of Crazy Snake." The unrealistic portrait of Chitto Harjo as a "noble red man" largely centers on an idealized physical type that includes references to Harjo's "eagle eye" and "stately mien." The caricature is undoubtedly drawn from his reading of Euro-American portrayals that idealized a lost Indian presence that never existed to begin with. The image of the "noble savage" was especially common in the late nineteenth century, and Posey certainly would have run across these unrealistic accounts in his extensive reading of newspapers, literary magazines, romantic poetry, and most definitely one of his favorite authors, Washington Irving. Posey's library contains ten of Irving's books, and in his journals Posey praises Irving as a writer who possesses the ability to write works of "wondrous beauty."[9] He even gave his first son the name Yahola Irving Posey. Many of Irving's

American Indians fall into the Rousseau-inspired idealized convention of virtuous, well-spoken, physically perfect children of nature. For example, in *The Sketchbook of Geoffrey Crayon*, Irving includes a piece entitled, "Traits of Indian Character," in which he writes:

> There is something in the character and habits of the North American savage, taken in connection with the scenery over which he is accustomed to range, its vast lakes, boundless forests, majestic rivers, and trackless plains, that is, to my mind, wonderfully striking and sublime. . . . His nature is stern, simple, and enduring; fitted to grapple with difficulties, and to support privations. . . . if we would but take the trouble to penetrate through that proud stoicism and habitual taciturnity.[10]

Though a reaction to earlier racist presentations of American Indians as ruthless demons of the wilderness, many view this "noble savage" portrayal as no less a form of racism because it trades one stereotype for another and ignores the reality of American Indian humanity, rights, and culture. As a member of a beleaguered American Indian nation, Posey had a front row seat to forms of malicious racism. Perhaps he so welcomed a seemingly positive view of his people that he allowed himself to ignore what he knew was a fictional cultural assessment. Thus, when presented with the dilemma of writing about his own people, he chose the representation he found most appealing and promoted it in his writing.

In Posey's "Journal of the Creek Enrollment Field Party" a complicated opinion of the Muscogee traditionalists emerges when he attempts to debate the issue of allotment with one of the leaders of the anti-allotment conservative group (also called the "Snakes"):

> John Kelly, is high in the "Snake" council and proposes to stand by the "old treaties" at all hazards. I approached him once while he was at work in his "sofky patch" and tried to explain to him the utter uselessness of holding out against the inevitable—how

the tribal governments had fallen into decay—how the country had been over-run by white people, outnumbering the Indians ten to one—how it was impossible for the United States to arrest progress in order that the Indians might enjoy undisturbed possession of their country.... But he would have none of it, saying, "The real Indian was not consulted as to allotment of lands; if he had been consulted he would have never consented to depart from the customs and traditions of his fathers. Our tribal government was upset by a stroke of the pen, because a few cried 'Change' and because we were helpless. I call myself a real Indian; you see me here today tilling my ground, tomorrow you will find me here. The real Indian does not change and is steadfast in the truth. He will not be reconciled to wrong. The government of the United States has made us solemn pledges and without our consent has no right to break them. As for us we will keep good faith." So spoke John Kelly and so he speaks today.[11]

This passage reveals Posey's view that the conservatives of his tribe adhered to doomed traditions and antiquated ideals. Yet even in describing this conversation, a discussion in which John Kelly argues that progressive Muscogees like Posey are not "real Indians," Posey maintains a form of romanticized admiration, a belief that some of his own people fit the mold of the "noble savage." The closing line, "So spoke John Kelly and so he speaks today," echoes the "proud stoicism and habitual taciturnity" found in Washington Irving's "Traits of Indian Character." While Posey believed that the conservatives of his nation led quaint but admirable lives, he also held that they could not survive in the rapidly changing world of Euro-American encroachment.

Despite its weaknesses, Posey's best writing bursts forth with vibrant, playful language that conjures a hopeful (if idealized) natural world. The same man who loved to walk in the meadows and woods that surrounded his homes at Bald Hill and in the Tulledegas also loved to create such places in his writing. His nature poems—especially those devoted to birds and the ubiquitous Oktahutche—repeatedly manage to call forth inventive lines and singing language that collectively represent a love letter written to the natural world as one could find it within the Muscogee Nation. For example, Posey's very brief poem "The Bluebird" works precisely because of its brevity: its straightforward yet striking image and simple delivery portray an Indian Territory sky found only in Posey's literary world. Another poem, "Autumn," stands as one of his major successes; the poem's apparently experimental character enhances the elements of what might otherwise be just another paean to the natural world. Its springing rhythm and warm imagery evoke the natural world not as a reflection of reality but as Posey wanted it to be—and as it remains in his verse. The best of Posey's nature poetry becomes a sort of Indian Territory pastoral that ranks with the best verse of the time.

Several poems serve as windows into Posey's unique Indian Territory setting, they echo Muscogee oral tradition, and they make direct references to his cultural influences. These poems—just as many of Posey's stories and journal entries—should be read as precious cultural gems. These poems, including "The Indian's Past Olympic" and several that were, until this edition, virtually unknown—such as "God and the Flying Squirrel (A Creek Legend)," "Fus Harjo and Old Billy Hell," "The Warrior's Dream," and "A Fable"—draw heavily upon Posey's Muscogee cultural traditions and cannot be measured by conventional Euro-American ideas of literary worth.

The cultural and literary implications of Alexander Posey's work remain fertile areas of research and appreciation and stand as keys to understanding the broader artistic sensibilities and concepts associated with both Muscogee literary identity and American Indian culture in general. Most of Posey's works have spent a century hidden and all but forgotten in archives. Now is the time to bring them into the light, to blow the dust from his words, and to give them the attention they deserve.

Notes

1. Daniel F. Littlefield Jr., *Alex Posey: Creek Poet, Journalist, and Humorist* (Lincoln: University of Nebraska Press, 1992), 2. Many of the biographical details given in this introduction originate from this source. For those seeking more information about Alexander Posey's life there is no better source than Littlefield's biography.

2. Charles Gibson, "Gone Over to See," *Indian Journal*, June 5, 1908.

3. Craig S. Womack, *Red on Red: Native American Literary Separatism* (Minneapolis: University of Minnesota Press, 1999), 133.

4. Minnie H. Posey letter to F. S. Barde, January 29, 1910, Frederick S. Barde Collection, Archives and Manuscripts Division, Oklahoma Historical Society.

5. For Posey's uncensored thoughts on religion see Posey, "Col. McIntosh: A Few Words to His Memory," in *Chinnubbie and the Owl: Muscogee (Creek) Stories, Orations, and Oral Traditions*, ed. Matthew Wynn Sivils (Lincoln: University of Nebraska Press, 2005), 92–94; and Littlefield, *Alex Posey*, 252–53.

6. Alexander Posey, quoted in William Elsey Connelley, "Memoir of Alexander Lawrence Posey," in *The Poems of Alexander Lawrence Posey*, collected and arranged by Mrs. Minnie H. Posey (Topeka: Crane, 1910), 61–62.

7. Quoted in Connelley, "Memoir."

8. Quoted in Connelley, "Memoir."

9. Alexander Posey, "Journal of the Creek Orphan Asylum," January 19, 1897, Alexander L. Posey Collection, folder 18, Gilcrease Museum, Tulsa, Oklahoma.

10. Washington Irving, "Traits of Indian Character," in *The Legend of Sleepy Hollow and Other Stories in the Sketch Book* (New York: Signet, 1981), 272.

11. Posey, "Journal of the Creek Enrollment Field Party," September 2, 1905, Alexander L. Posey Collection, folder 38, Gilcrease Museum, Tulsa, Oklahoma.

Song of the Oktahutche

[Take my valentine and be]

Take my valentine and be
More than all the world to me.
Take me too and then my heart,
From your love shall never part
Take my purse and let it hold,   5
All your wealth in stocks and gold;
Give me love and wealth combined
And I will be your Valentine.

Manuscript dated February 14, 1891, folder 77, Alexander L. Posey Collection, Gilcrease Museum, Tulsa, Oklahoma. The back of the manuscript reads "Mr. A. Posey."

The Warrior's Dream

    Wounded on the battle-field I lay,
Neglected there and cast away;
By arrows pierced, no friend to see;
Alone in solitude and agony:
Without a hope to comfort me,   5
Save my anxious hopes of eternity.
Left to treach'rous chance and fate,
To die and knock at Hell's or Heaven's gate.
Around me heaped the decomposing dead,
And horrors filled my dreams with dread.   10
The solemn form of melancholy stood
Or lurk'd about to bathe its feet in blood.
    The silent braves lay lifeless side by side,
With them my nation's hope of conquest died—
Pluck'd as a bloom in Summer's prime,   15
And doomed to fall long ere its time.
Their locks uncrowned by Winter's age—
The glossy prize of manhood's stage,
Stream'd in the sighing zephyr's breath,
As if no orbless gloom infested death.   20
As if the queen of future hopes was nigh,
But sleep had seal'd each warrior's eye,
The avenger's key had lock'd their tomb—
Thus back to earth—their mother's womb.
Eternal silence paused and all was still,   25
And not a note or sound the woods did fill,
As the sinking beams of day declined
The western waves and heights behind.

The silver queen of night drew back the blinds
Of the eastern void and kiss'd the mournful pines.   30
What grandeurs smiled, what beauteous scenes!
But lo, on yonder corpse, the savage tiger gleans,
And curls his ruthless lips in scorn,
The ghastly form beneath his paw is torn.
Oh, wondrous man! thou king of Earth!   35
Born to increase an animal's mirth!
And all thy joys doth swiftly pass
In a few days, then gone, alas!
    An arrow thro' my cheeks had sped
Its viewless course and I in torrents bled;   40
Naught was I but mangled flesh,
For jaws of heartless dogs to crush,
And hourly nearing swift decay—
In bonds of woe and pain I lay.
'Twas vain to hope, 'twas vain to pray,   45
In manhood's prime my head was gray.
Denied by springs, rivers and rain,
And even dew, I thirst in pain.
No food was nigh to tempt my eyes,
Save flesh that wolves and vultures prize.   50
    How strange is human destiny!
What miseries pay existence's fee!
This truth did rack and haunt my brain
Till I no longer wished for life again,
And wonder'd how in want and pain   55
I lived while counted with the slain.
'Tis strange I thought, but lo, I found,
The Water-god had coiled around
To shield me from fatigue and harm:
I reached to him my quivering arm   60
And begged for death or liberty—

For life or in the tomb to be.
Of his presence I was scarce aware,
When I was lifted mountain heights in air,
On curls of azure fume, the most divine
That rose above the Sea-god's shrine.
Behold! my wounded form was gone,
And viewless as the winds I rode upon,
Yet my thoughts and happy feelings had,
And I tho' marv'ling much was glad.
My wish was answered, as I asked—
My soul by pain no longer tasked;
Could think and see and loudly talk,
And move at will and proudly walk.
I saw below my place of woe
And somber mountains wrapped in snow—
The mangled dead were dim to view,
As I passed the azure heavens thro'.
The Sun and Moon, I left behind,
And came to starry worlds sublime,
In which unfading summer reigned—
And love and rapturous mirths unnamed.
Past countless worlds and journeyed on
And on to brighter worlds anon
And anchor'd safe in Heaven's harbor great;
The home of peace, the soul's estate.
I met the gods and praised them all,
My former friends and warriors tall;
Gazed on radiant structures grand,
And all the gems of glory's land.
The Earth was hell when matched with these,
Where shackling death no life can seize.
On emerald thrones and evergreen,
Sat the gods the ivory walls between;

And herds of bison white as polar's snow 95
Were the roaming target of the warrior's bow.
As silver threads of brightest dye,
The rivers crooked and pass'd me by.
The dazzling domes of crystal mountains rose
Unknown to the savage winds and Winter's foes, 100
There leap'd the roe and laugh'd the warrior bold,
There blush'd the rose tho' endless ages roll'd.
And circumfused in various tints of gold,
Did ballad-kings their tuneful lyres hold.
No days there were nor sable nights; 105
No weeks, no months, nor yearly flights;
No sleep, no death, no ill nor pains;
No want, nor woes that Earth contains.
    When rosy morn again had beamed
Its orient light I thus had dreamed, 110
And this foretold my future fall:
The ocean's brood did my home enthrall,
And hurled my youthful bloom
To death and dark eternal gloom.
My dream of Heaven's paradise, 115
Forbade my land and warrior's rise.
My wilds, the soil that gave me birth—
My woes and grief the world might girth,
Or reach to stars my dream hath seen,
Beyond the fiery Sun that rolls between. 120
What woes infest a nation's path!
Whose end is tears though born to laugh!
This dream inscribed my epitaph!

B.I.U. Instructor, June 16, 1892, George J. Mitchell Department of Special Collections and Archives, Bowdoin College Library, Brunswick, Maine.

[And old or new, can records find]

And old or new, can records find
    A nobler man in book or scroll,
Than he who taught a nation's mind
    To love the freedom of the soul

Fragment of a longer poem (now lost) in praise of Thomas Paine. Posey to Remsburg, November 25, 1892, "Letters Written by A. L. Posey and Charles Gibson," Archives and Manuscripts Division, Oklahoma Historical Society.

Line 2: According to a November 25, 1892, letter from Posey to George J. Remsburg, the "nobler man" refers to Thomas Paine (1737–1809), whose political writings such as *Common Sense* and *The Crisis* championed American independence from Britain and whose longer works, *The Rights of Man* and *The Age of Reason*, promoted Paine's deism and concern with civil rights. Posey much admired Thomas Paine and alludes to Paine's *The Crisis* in his oration "The Creek Opening Guns;" see Posey, *Chinnubbie and the Owl*, 99.

Death of the Poets

Lowell first, then Whitman, Whittier went;
Next, the lyric bards of songs—the
English laureate. Who to
Follow them? Our Wendell Holmes?
Then, alas! the space and sky their   5
Genius lit must darken to its stars!
How long, oh, will the shadow last?—
Until as bright or brighter orbs
Appear, and flood the realms of rhyme,—
Celestial, glowing, newly born!   10
Yes, the poetic sky is scant of suns,
And only by its minor beacons graced
But 'tis true, unbidden wonders come
And meteors flash, and Sol at eve is
Sinking but to rise.   15

Typescript by Daniel F. Littlefield Jr. of a newspaper clipping now missing from the Gilcrease; Littlefield Collection, ANPA.

Line 1: James Russell Lowell (1819–1891), Walt Whitman (1819–1892), and John Greenleaf
    Whittier (1807–1892).
Line 3: Alfred, Lord Tennyson (1809–1892) was the English laureate.
Line 4: This poem appears to date from the period before Oliver Wendell Holmes's death
    on October 7, 1894. As the clipping of this poem (now lost) was noted as bearing
    the typeface of the *B.I.U. Instructor*, it probably dates from around 1893 when Posey
    worked at that paper.

Red Man's Pledge of Peace [circa 1893]

I pledge you by the moon and sun,
As long as stars their course shall run,
Long as day shall meet my view,
Peace shall reign between us two.

As long as grass shall clothe the fields, 5
As long as earth her bounty yields,
I this saying ne'er will rue:
Peace shall reign between us two.

Lo! Indian tribes of times unborn
Shall ne'er this sacred treaty scorn— 10
Or in arms seek war with you—
Peace shall reign between us two.

I came from mother soil and cave,
You came from pathless sea and wave,
Strangers fought our battles thro'— 15
Peace shall reign between us two.

As long as eagles wing their flight
Above their mountain eyrie's height,
Long as years their youth renew,
Peace shall reign between us two. 20

As long as streams to oceans flow,
As long as seasons come and go,
Long as truth is truth and true,
Peace shall reign between us two.

We met as foes, we part as friends;   25
Now mildly earth and ocean blends,
Clasping hands we bid adieu—
Peace shall reign between us two.

Typescript by Daniel F. Littlefield of a newspaper clipping now missing from the Gilcrease; Littlefield Collection, ANPA. On this typescript Littlefield notes that the clipping of this poem bore the typeface of the *B.I.U. Instructor*, and the poem probably dates from around 1893 when Posey worked on that paper. In 1898 Posey revised this poem, and another version appears in folder 140 of the Gilcrease Posey Collection. These two later versions immediately follow this one.

Line 13: According to the Muscogee (Creek) creation myth, those people who would eventually become Muscogees first emerged from a cave. See Chaudhuri and Chaudhuri, *A Sacred Path*, 14–22.

Red Man's Pledge of Peace [circa 1898]

I pledge you by the moon and sun,
As long as stars their course shall run,
Long as day shall meet my view,
Peace shall reign between us two.

I pledge you by those peaks of snow, 5
As long as streams to ocean flow,
Long as years their youth renew,
Peace shall reign between us two.

I came from mother soil and cave,
You came from pathless sea and wave, 10
Strangers fought our battles through,—
Peace shall reign between us two.

An undated manuscript on Superintendent of Public Instruction stationery, folder 123, Posey Collection, Gilcrease. For more information see the source note for *Red Man's Pledge of Peace* [circa 1893].

Red Man's Pledge of Peace [ledger version]

I pledge you by the moon and the sun,
As long as stars their course shall run,
Long as day shall meet my view,
Peace shall reign between us two.

Lo! Indian tribes of times unborn   5
Shall ne'er this sacred treaty scorn—
Or in arms seek war with you—
Peace shall reign between us two.

I came from mother soil and cave,
You came from pathless sea and wave,   10
Strangers fought our battles through,—
Peace shall reign between us two.

I pledge you by those peaks of snow,
As long as streams to ocean flow,
Long as years their youth renew,   15
Peace shall reign between us two.

Ledger, folder 140, Posey Collection, Gilcrease. For more information see the source note for *Red Man's Pledge of Peace* [circa 1893].

The Burial of the Alabama Prophet

Slow moves the fun'ral train,
    No trumpet sounds are heard;
The dead's forth-borne in pain,
    In sorrow, grief interred.

No lays of death are sung,   5
    No pompous scenes are made,
No praise of mortal tongue,
    No sacred rites are paid.

Last duties to the dead
    Are paid in silent tears;   10
No words are lisped or said—
    The coffin disappears.

Sad-lowered to his cell
    With hopes of life beyond,
Exempt from fears of hell—   15
    No marble decks his mound.

For, he, when dying, said,
    "I wish no lips to praise
The life that I have led,
    Nor hands my tomb to raise.   20

"Let Time his tribute pay.
    With flow'ring seasons 'bove
The form returned to clay
    Whose deeds were human love.

"Far better there to sleep　　　　　　　　　　　25
　　　The endless sleep of death,
Where vines and mosses creep,
　　　Than tombs of gold beneath.

"At eve, when sinks the sun,
　　　Its tomb's in ev'ry heart;　　　　　　　　30
Wherefore erect ME one,
　　　When death bids me depart?

"O life, farewell—I go,
　　　And leave this earthly tide;
'Tis sweet and well to know　　　　　　　　　35
　　　'Tis rest in death to 'bide."

Now wild-wood's turf below,
　　　Where footsteps seldom tread,
Where thick'ning forests grow
　　　And oaks their branches spread,　　　　40

In Nature's clasp and care—
　　　In life's last still retreat—
A sleep that all must share,
　　　Lies one whose work's complete.

Sleep on thou mighty one,　　　　　　　　　　45
　　　Thro' time and distant years,
Because of what thou'st done,
　　　Thy name shall live in tears!

Undated pamphlet, scrapbook, Posey Collection, Gilcrease. The back of this pamphlet has an ornament composed of a scythe, stalks of grain, and a flower, and reads: "PUBLISHED BY INDIAN UNIVERSITY, Bacone, Ind. Ter."

Twilight [Eventide]

Beyond the far-off waves the seagulls cry,
    As twilight shades
    The emerald glades
And zephyrs waft the strains of nightbirds nigh,
    Now sinks the sun—
    Its course is run—
    The day is done—
It fades in the gold of the western sky.

Now high, in raven files, the must'ring crows
    Their wings display,
    Thro' ether way,
And transient gleams and saffron bars disclose,
    And beauties throng
    The sky along;
    And bugs of song
Now pipe among the vales of dew-kissed rose.

Now Night, on high, her spangled robe unfurls,
    Unveils the moon—
    The silver moon—
The orbs, the milky ways, the circling worlds:
    Now bright, sublime
    In clusters shine
    The stars divine,
And 'cross the twinkling void the meteor whirls.

Undated pamphlet, scrapbook, Posey Collection, Gilcrease. This poem is typeset in the style of Bacone Indian University publications and was published as "Eventide" in the 1910 edition of Posey's poems. A manuscript of this poem is in folder 140 of the Gilcrease Posey Collection.

[Autumn days—bright days of gold]

Autumn days—bright days of gold;
Ah! lovely, filled with cheer!
Not, as one has said of old,
    "The saddest of the year."

Photocopy of an undated clipping from *Indian Journal*, [October 1893], box 1-22.6, Littlefield Collection, ANPA. Though this clipping lacks a date, it may have been published in 1893 because it originates from one of Posey's short Bacone Indian University articles for the *Indian Journal*. In the article Posey writes, "Indian University opened its doors, Monday, October 2nd, to a large number of students." As October 2 fell on a Monday in 1893, Posey probably published this piece that year, perhaps in middle or late October.

Line 4: A quotation from William Cullen Bryant's poem "The Death of the Flowers." The first two lines of the poem read: "The Melancholy days have come, the saddest of the year, / Of wailing winds, and naked woods, and meadows brown and sere."

Death of a Window Plant

The air was chill,
The leaves were hushed,
    The moon in grandeur
Climbed the spangled
Walls of heaven, 5
    When the angel came
That whispers death;
Unseen, unheard,
    To lisp that word and
Leave my window 10
Sad when night should
    Blossom into day.
The moon had waned,
And each bright star,
    Like visions of a 15
Dream. Up rose the
Sun on wings of
    Gold, and soared thro' fields
Of light serene;
All earth seemed gay, 20
    And banished from it,
Sorrow; birds sang
Songs of summer
    In the clear sweet sky.
But I was sad, 25
And song of bird
    Nor sky of splendor
Could for one brief

Moment bring a
    Solace to my heart.
I mourned, and all
Was dark and drear
    Within my chamber,
Lorn and bare, where
Sweetness was and
    Beauty for a day.
My window-friend,
I'll dig thy grave,
    Inter thee grandly,
No sod shall lay
Nor blossom there
    Thy kindred flowers.
Within my soul's
Deep core is built
    Thy tomb enduring.
Ah, morn shall kiss
Thee nevermore
    In purple of dawn;
And stars shall rise
And twinkle in
    Vain and pass away.
Should all thy race
Thus disappear,
    In death forsake the
Soil in which you
Grew, the world would
    Then be sad as I.

Photocopy of a clipping set in *B.I.U. Instructor* type, box 1-22.11, Littlefield Collection, ANPA. William Elsey Connelley mentions that this poem derives from a January 1894 issue of the *B.I.U. Instructor*, but no copy has been found. See Connelley, "Memoir of Alexander Lawrence Posey," in Minnie H. Posey, comp., *The Poems of Alexander Lawrence Posey* (Topeka: Crane and Company, 1910), 20.

O, Oblivion!

O, Oblivion, how thou'rt robbed and cheated!
Congress never meets but there is seated
From thy dark abode some politician
With a bill anent the demolition
Of our Indian governments, and gets in   5
Print, like Curtis and the well-named Dennis Flynn,
And that there man from Colorado—Teller,
I believe, he's called—that wondrous feller
Who thundered by us once aboard a car,
And knew just what was needed here, by Gar!   10
But Dawes will make thee restitution,
Though he violates the Constitution!

Undated clipping, scrapbook, Posey Collection, Gilcrease. The subject matter of this poem probably dates it to 1894 when the Dawes Commission first began work in Indian Territory.

Line 6: Charles Curtis (1860–1936), a prominent politician from Kansas, introduced the Curtis Act in 1896, which called for the allotment of Indian Territory lands to individual members of the Five Tribes (Cherokee, Muscogee [Creek], Chickasaw, Choctaw, and Seminole). The Curtis Act eventually passed in 1898, paving the way for the dissolution of tribal governments and Oklahoma statehood. A congressional delegate from Pennsylvania, Dennis T. Flynn (1861–1939), advocated the incorporation of Indian Territory into the proposed state of Oklahoma. Many American Indians, Posey included, hoped that Indian Territory would become a separate state.

Line 7: The Colorado Senator, Henry Moore Teller (1830–1914), had been the source of an infamously shoddy account of the supposedly poor condition of life in Indian Territory. His report helped fuel the argument that the United States should absorb Indian Territory.

Line 11: Both a Massachusetts congressman and a senator during his political career, Henry Laurens Dawes (1816–1903) served as the head of the congressional commission charged with persuading the Five Tribes to abandon their own governments and to accept the allotment of land in severalty.

Ye Men of Dawes

Ye men of Dawes, avaunt!
    Return from whence ye came!
If ye are godly men—
        I fear ye're not the same—
        Lay down this work of shame!   5
        This first thing that ye know
Five thous'n' will warp
    Your little conscience so!

Is there no good that ye
    Can do in any state   10
That ye have come among
        Us, so precipitate,
        For to negotiate?
Lo! has the lurid flame
Of mobs gone out at last,   15
With crimes by every name?

O man of Dawes, ye talk
    As sleek as ratpaths 'neath
A crib, or slipp'ry elm
        Tree growing on the heath;   20
        Ye all take lodgings, faith,
        In manner to impress:
Look kind o' sour, as if
    In mighty mental stress:

Ye wear duck suits galore   25
    And shoes of patent skin:

> Ye strut majestically;
> > But ye can't lead us in
> > To any such a sin
> > As giving aid to ye 30
> To sanctify a wrong—
> > Gives robbery chastity!

Undated clipping, scrapbook, Posey Collection, Gilcrease. This clipping is signed "Shimubbie Harjo," and is probably a typesetter's misreading of Posey's "Chinnubbie Harjo" signature, which boasts a capital "C" that in some manuscripts resembles an "S." The subject matter of this poem probably dates it to 1894, when the Dawes Commission first began work in Indian Territory.

Line 1: In 1893 a United States congressional committee chaired by Henry Laurens Dawes created the Dawes Act, which allowed for the formation of the Dawes Commission. This commission was charged with facilitating the dissolution of tribal land titles and providing for the allotment of land in severalty to the individual members of the so-called Five Civilized Tribes (i.e., the Muscogee [Creek], Cherokee, Chickasaw, Choctaw, and Seminole Nations).

[Did'st thou see the spectral blossoms fall?]

Did'st thou see the spectral blossoms fall?
And heard'st thou the north winds moan and shriek and sigh?
Did'st thou see bright heaps of snow 'gainst the wall,
On meadow, tree and hill, and drift and dazzle by?

Photocopy of an undated clipping from *Indian Journal*, circa 1894, box I-22.6, Littlefield Collection, ANPA. Though this clipping lacks a date, it (as well as "[Oh, those voices now we hear]" and "[Forsooth, thou art so versatile, O Bob!]") may have been published in 1894 because it opens one of Posey's short Bacone Indian University articles for the *Indian Journal*, most of which date from that year.

[Oh, those voices now we hear]

Oh, those voices now we hear,
    So gladdening, cheery, ye,
How quaint and strange,
    Oh, those faces prize we dear,
And though we laugh, we marvel at the change!

Photocopy of an undated clipping from *Indian Journal*, circa 1894, box 1-22.6, Littlefield Collection, ANPA.

[Forsooth, thou art so versatile, O Bob!]

Forsooth, thou art so versatile, O Bob!
And naught, in which we fail alike and sob
To know our weakness, never baffles thee
'Twas nature's kind intent that thou shouldst be
A horseman, fireman, tiller of the land,
A doctor, scholar, speaker, singer grand;
And higher, nobler yet than all of these,
A bard, whose measured thoughts doth greatly please!

Photocopy of an undated clipping from *Indian Journal*, January 30, [1894?], box 1-22.6, Littlefield Collection, ANPA.

[To allot, or not to allot]

To allot, or not to allot, that is the
Question; whether 'tis nobler in the mind to
Suffer the country to lie in common as it is,
Or to divide it up and give each man
His share pro rata, and by dividing   5
End this sea of troubles? To allot, divide,
Perchance to end in statehood;
Ah, there's the rub!

Indian Journal, March 1, 1894. This poem is obviously a satirical allusion to the famous soliloquy from Shakespeare's *Hamlet* and demonstrates how the young poet incorporated his literary influences into statements about the political environment of Indian Territory.

[For two long days the polar breeze]

For two long days the polar breeze
    Blew swift and crisp and cool,
The buds are dead upon the trees,
    And frogs have left the pool.

The birds have ceased to twitter sweet
    Spring songs, 'Tis sad, alas!
And ev'rywhere you trod you meet
    The vi'let on the grass.

And daisy lying drooped and dead,
    The poet lorn surveys
The sylvan scene where late he said,
    "O, Spring, 'tis thee I praise!"

Indian Journal, March 29, 1894.

[The picnic's coming]

The picnic's coming,
Strawberries rip'ning,
The May is passing,
And the June will bring
Three months of rest and joy and ease, 5
Three months of doing as you please.

Indian Journal, May 11, 1894.

[The whippowill has come]

The whippowill has come
    To chant his dreamy lay;
The bumble-bees now hum
    Thro' all the lovely day,
The man with books to sell 5
    Now knocks upon your door—
And you could quickly fell
    Him welt'ring in his gore.

Indian Journal, May 25, 1894.

[Those bursts of oratory—how they stir the soul!]

Those bursts of oratory—how they stir the soul!
Demosthenes, arise, that you may hear them roll
Like thunder-peals among the Alpine
Steeps, and mock that tongue of dust of thine!

Indian Journal, June 8, 1894.

Line 2: Considered by some as the greatest of the Greek orators, Demosthenes (384?–322 BC) gained notoriety through a series of orations called the *Philippics* and *Olynthiacs* which called for Greeks to fight against Macedonian tyranny. Posey, an accomplished orator himself, perhaps saw a parallel between the situation of the Greeks during Demosthenes's day and the political atmosphere of Indian Territory.

Wildcat Bill

Whoop a time er two fer me!
    Turn me loose an' let be be!
I'm Wildcat Bill,
    From Grizzle Hill,
A border ranger; never down'd;   5
    A western hero all around:
A gam'bler, scalper, born a scout;
    A tough; the man ye read about,
From no man's lan';
    Kin' rope a bear an' ride a buck;   10
Git full on booze an' run amuck;
    Afeard o' nothin'; hard to beat;
Kin die with boots upon my feet—
    An' like a man!

Indian Journal, December 14, 1894.

Line 9: With Kansas's western boundary located at the 37th parallel and the conditions of the Missouri Compromise forbidding Texas (a slave state) to claim any land above 36° 30′ North, a small strip of unclaimed land between the two states came into existence. This thirty-four-mile-wide and 128-mile-long piece of land came to be called "No Man's Land" and would, in 1890, become incorporated into Oklahoma Territory (and now forms Beaver County in western Oklahoma).

There's a Tide

There's a tide in the lives of men
    Which, when taken at its flood,
Will land a fellow's bark of life
    To the quarter-deck in mud,

There's a tide in the lives of men 5
    Which, when taken at its ebb,
Will strand the lubber's crazy craft
    In the sharper's fatal web.

Then what the deuce's a fellow to do
    In life's queer navigation— 10
Must he be tossed by every squall
    And beat by all creation?

No, gentle reader; follow me,
    And by the Great Eternal,
You'll get the inside tack on life— 15
    Just read the INDIAN JOURNAL.

Indian Journal, March 1, 1895. The authorship of this poem is unconfirmed, but Posey is probably the author because of the poem's style, literary allusion, and humor.

Line 2: The opening lines of the first and second stanza are puns drawn from Shakespeare's *Julius Caesar* (IV.3.218).

Line 8: Another term for a swindler.

Line 16: The Eufaula *Indian Journal* was a newspaper that Posey kept in close association with for much of his life. He worked on the paper as a young student and then went on to write for and edit the paper in later years.

[In UNCLE SAM'S dominion]

In UNCLE SAM'S dominion
    A few own all the "dust."
They rule by combination
    And trade by forming trusts.

In the "injun's" own arrangement
    We acknowledge with a sigh,
We can realize derangement.
    Tho' the moat is in our eye.

But in trying to reform us,
    Our great white Uncle, why
Don't you firstly pluck the saw-log
    From out your own black eye?

Indian Journal, March 1, 1895. The authorship of this poem is unconfirmed, but Posey is probably the author because the poem's style, literary allusion, and humor.

Lowyna

The lark,
From dawn
Till dark,
Has drawn,
On fence and post and tree, 5
    In meadow, brown and sere,
From out its heart, so free,
So full of mirth and glee,
Sweet songs of ecstasy,
    To hail the glad new year 10
That makes you twenty-three!

Manuscript dated February 3, 1896, on Creek Orphan Asylum stationery, folder 80, Posey Collection, Gilcrease. The title refers to Posey's pet name for his wife, Minnie Harris Posey (born on February 3, 1873). Minnie Posey explained in a letter to Edward Everett Dale that the name meant "loving the bright and happy." See Minnie H. Posey to Edward Everett Dale, February 19, 1919, Dale Collection, Western History Collection, University of Oklahoma, Norman. Posey would later alter the spelling to "Lowena."

The Indian's Past Olympic

The gala day has come—'tis morn;
In mounds high heaps the rip'ning corn,
Which warriors dare not touch, disdain
Till now, and bisons from the plain,
Wild turkeys, bears and antelopes
From shady wilds and mountain slopes,
And meats from all the woods around,
Doth grace the ancient, sacred ground,
Where painted nations group in one
To shout the praise of battles won.
And lo! 'tis half of heaven's bliss
To see a scene as grand as this:
Now squaws begin the meat to roast,
And all shall now enjoy the toast;
The prophet, plumed, slow taps the drum,
Exclaims aloud: "O Warriors come
And drink this noble drink I give,
And thus prolong the years you live,
As did your fathers, slumb'ring sound
Beneath the soil—their native ground.
Cleanse well your souls of former sin
And all the vile that lurks within;
Begin anew, as doth the year
And young you'll be when death is near."

This said, the prophet taps the drum,
And music rings—tum, tum, tum, tum,
The ball is tossed, thro' air serene,

With speed, it flies on wings unseen.
With ball-sticks pointing to the skies
Each warrior stands with watchful eyes;　　　　　30
And like a thunderbolt that's hurled
From heaven downward to the world,
Hard strikes the ball upon the ground,
And gives the ear its muffled sound.
The warriors whoop and whooping bound　　　　35
As lions on the shepherd's pen,
Loud blends the shouts of savage men.

Each strikes and striking seeks his end;
True friendship's lost and foes contend.
High to and fro the ball is thrown,　　　　　　40
And gaping wounds by war clubs torn,
Gush torrents, streams of clotting gore,
The thirsty earth fast spreading o'er.
And now, anon, like winds at sea,
When typhoons, raging storms are free,　　　　45
Rush rank on rank, more swift, intense
In fury's maddened violence!
In mis'ry, pain, remorse untold
Lies groaning, foiled the warrior bold—
Unquenched his thirst, unkissed his lips,　　　50
Unmourned his fate—death angel grips
The valiant form, the lifeless brave
And wings him, sleeping, to his grave;
Uncoffined there and left alone,
To dust returning, bone by bone.　　　　　　　55
And not one drop of tear is shed,
Or words of grief or sorrow said
By those who watch or those who play,
Where men their kindreds, fellows slay.

The victor wins the victor's name, 60
And honors great enhance his fame;
Becomes he chief and warrior bold—

'Tis past—the tragic scene is told.
"Now bathe ye braves and swift prepare
And feast we now in twilight air!" 65
In tones aloud the prophet speaks.
And now a pool each warrior seeks
And bathes his gory form and scars
Beneath the gleaming twilight stars.
Lo! gorgeous heaps of flesh are spread, 70
And piles of most delicious bread
Which scent the straying zephyrs round:
Each warrior's seated on the ground,
And smiling maids their wants supply,
While howls the wolf and jackals cry 75
Upon the lifeless and the slain,
Left tombless on the battle-plain—
Enough to freeze the human veins!
Yet pleasure, joy and laughter reigns;
And lo! 'tis naught but earthly bliss 80
To them, inured to sights like this.

The moon is up, most lovely night!
The center flame is blazing bright,
And war-whoops peal from crag to crag,
Adown the hollow cavern's swag 85
And on the wave of waters near,
To hills repeating as they hear.
Now round and about the blaze
Revives the sport of other days.
Each ankle of the maiden race 90
A snowy tortoise shell doth grace,

And brilliant plumes the warrior's head,
Who, like the haughty peacock, spread
Their vast and gleamy plumage round,
Pretentious sweep and court the ground. 95
The prophet shakes the hollow gourd
In which are stones and pebbles stored,
To cheer, enthuse the rev'ling band;
And, lifting high his jeweled hand
Exclaims the leader, "Heap the flame— 100
As burns the blaze so burns our fame!"
And fiery sparks, like met'ors, rush
High upward thro' the woods and brush,
Revealing all the savage host,
Of life regardless, and its cost; 105
Eyes like burnished em'ralds gleaming—
Strange in form—as demons seeming.

Full in the zenith beams the moon,
'Tis midnight's melancholy noon,
So clear, serene, so pure and bright. 110
The met'or wings his burning flight
And, flashing dies upon his way.
'Tis lovely—grander far than day.
The ghosts of mountains spread around
And peaks, by snows of ages crowned, 115
Look down upon the rev'ling host
In savage bliss and pleasures lost,
Fast circling round the center-blaze.
The prophets chant their battle-lays,
And tap the muffled drums to bass 120
The songs and speed the warrior's pace.
They pause, they stop, but not for dreams—
For brighter still the pine-light gleams,

And mortal sleep now hath no charms
'Mid rapture, war-whoop's loud alarms. 125
Their strength refreshed and thirst allayed
A rush, a thundering rush is made
To gain the ring, the beaten ground.
And now again they circle round
And sing aloud of battles won; 130
The deeds of mighty chieftains done.
The sky is changed, and now 'tis gray—
The luna-orb has lost its way.
Day blossoms crimson in the east
And ends the dance, the play and feast. 135

Muskogee Phoenix, December 17, 1896. As this poem is signed "A. L. Posey" instead of the more common "Chinnubbie Harjo," it may date from Posey's earlier Bacone poems, which were long and often bore his real name.

Line 1: Much of this poem describes the traditional Muscogee stickball game that typically occurs during the annual Green Corn Ceremony. Stickball games are often played between rival towns and sometimes become quite violent. The game is called "little brother of war" and involves maneuvering a ball toward the rival goal with a club-like racket. See Wright, *Creeks and Seminoles*, 21, and Debo, *Road to Disappearance*, 25–26.

Line 15: A "prophet" is a Muscogee medicine man, or *hilis haya*. See Chaudhuri and Chaudhuri, *A Sacred Path*, 118–19 and Wright, *Creeks and Seminoles*, 157–60. For an extended discussion of the role of the Muscogee medicine man see Lewis and Jordan, *Creek Indian Medicine Ways*.

Line 17: A reference to the ingestion of sacred medicine, possibly the medicine called "ussi" or "black drink." See Lewis and Jordan, *Creek Indian Medicine Ways*, 6.

Line 91: A reference to the turtle shell rattles that women "shell-shakers" use when performing ceremonial dances. See Wright, *Creeks and Seminoles*, 38.

Cuba Libre

Forward, Cuba, forward!
    Down with treachery!
Forward! Hang the coward
    For his butchery!—
        Weyler, beast of Spain!   5

Forward! forward ever!
    Down with tyranny!
Forward! backward never
    From thy enemy!—
        Weyler beast of Spain!   10

On! on! Gomez, triumphantly!
Thou hast the wide world's sympathy!

Maceo, rest thee,
Cuba shall be free!

Muskogee Phoenix, December 24, 1896. A manuscript of this poem is in folder 140 of the Gilcrease Posey Collection.

Line 1: This poem advocates Cuba's struggle to gain independence from Spain, a cause that would escalate into the Spanish-American War in 1898.

Line 5: General Valeriano Weyler (1838–1930) was the Spanish governor of Cuba who, in an effort to keep rebels soldiers from hiding within the peaceful civilian population, relocated much of the population to camps. These camps were poorly conceived, and unhealthy conditions led to the death of thousands of people, many of them women and children.

Line 11: Máximo Gómez Baez (1836–1905) was one of the leaders of the military rebellion against Spain and helped engineer the hit and run guerilla tactics that were the trademark of the rebels.

Line 13: Antonio Maceo (1845–1896) was a popular commander of the Cuban Liberation Army which fought to free Cuba from Spanish rule.

Callie

It was April, and the orchard looked like
White clouds huddled up together, tightly
Tinged with crimson, accounting every zephyr
Callie, leaning from the window, begged in
Vain that afternoon for just a single   5
Blossom of the many in my hand. How
Gloriously pretty! and my love was
Deep for Callie; but a boyish heart was
Mine, and I had not the courage then to
offer any token of affection.   10
And, as, she sat there begging; and I stood
There hesitating, with my flowers; all
The while the martins sallied to and fro
Above us; all around the woods were green,
With here and there a glimpse of prairie land   15
Beyond; and still beyond, the mountains blue,
With cool dark shadows crawling over them.

Undated manuscript on Creek Orphan Asylum stationery, folder 92, Posey Collection, Gilcrease.

Mother and Baby

Tired at length of crying,
Laughing, cooing, sighing,
The baby lies so qui't and still,
    Scarce breathing in his sleep;
The mother watches half-inclined   5
    To hide her face and weep.

Undated manuscript on Creek Orphan Asylum stationery, folder 94, Posey Collection, Gilcrease. Another manuscript of this poem, with a third line that reads "The baby lies so calm and still," is in folder 140 of the Gilcrease Posey Collection.

Daisy

Mirthful Daisy,
    Pretty brindle pup;
Playful Daisy,
    Ever pricking up

Your ears to see
    The way the rabbit's gone.
    Or to accept a bone,
Impatiently;

Barking Daisy,
    Mischief-making pup;
Restless Daisy,
    Long the buttercup

Has watched you sleep.
    If there are squirrels there,
    In Heaven where you are—
        You went there when you died—
    Or cotton-tailed hare,
Or any sheep,
    The angels keep you tied!

But I am jesting.
    You were a friend, and true;
    A closer brother, too,
        Than some who've shook my hand.
    You ever gave alarm
    At ev'ry sign of harm.
        You were so faithful and—
I leave you resting.

Photocopy of an undated clipping, box 1-22.6, Littlefield Collection, ANPA. An apparently earlier manuscript of this poem is in folder 140 of the Gilcrease Posey Collection and matches this published version except for the first five lines, which read: "Playful Daisy, / Pretty brindle pup; / Watchful Daisy, / Ever perking up / . . . / Your sure to see." Posey mentions submitting "Daisy" for publication in a May 3, 1897, journal entry, meaning that the earliest version of the poem was written before that date. A truncated version of this poem entitled "On a Mischievous Pup" can be found as an undated newspaper clipping in an undated scrapbook in the Gilcrease.

The Squatter's Fence

He sets his posts so far apart
And tacks his barbed wire so slack
In haste to get the [Injun] land
Enclosed and squat him qui'lly down,
Unseen by any, that 5
His fence when built looks like
A country candy pulling!

Undated manuscript, folder 156, Posey Collection, Gilcrease. As this manuscript also contains a poetry fragment that would later become the first stanza of the poem "Sea Shells," this manuscript probably dates to before December 23, 1897, when "Sea Shells" was published in the *Muskogee Phoenix*.

The Conquerors

The Caesars and the Alexanders were
But men gone mad; who ran about a while
Upsetting kingdoms; and were slain in turn
Like rabid dogs, or died in misery.
Assassins laid in wait for Caesar; wine,   5
Amid the boasts of victory, cut short
The glory of the Macedonians;
Deception cooled the fever Pompey had;
Death was dealt to Pyrrhus by a woman's
Hand; Themistocles and Hannibal drank
Deep of poison in their desolation.   10

Manuscript dated January 13, 1897, on Creek Orphan Asylum stationery, folder 81, Posey Collection, Gilcrease. Another manuscript of this poem is in folder 140 of the Gilcrease Posey Collection.

Line 1: Gaius Julius Caesar (100–44 BC) was a Roman statesman who initiated the Roman imperial system. He was assassinated by a group of senators who feared his popularity would make him a king. Alexander the Great (356–323 BC), Macedonian king who conquered the Persian Empire.

Line 8: Gnaeus Pompeius Magnus (106–48 BC) was a Roman general and statesman who was a rival of Caesar.

Line 9: Pyrrhus (318?–272 BC), King of Epirus, supposedly died during a street skirmish when a woman threw a tile at him from the roof of a house. Themistocles (527?–460? BC) was an Athenian naval general and statesman who commanded the Athenian fleet at the Battle of Salamis. Legend has it he committed suicide by drinking poison. Hannibal (247–183 BC) was a Carthaginian general who famously crossed the Alps from Spain to attack Rome. Later in his career, with his capture by Roman forces imminent, Hannibal committed suicide by drinking poison.

Lines to Hall

You cannot sing in walls of brick,
    George Hall; go get thee to a hut
Along some Tulledegan creek.
    High life ill suits thy muse. Go put

Her up an altar on the moor,   5
    And keep the robins company.
You're not yourself when not obscure
    From gaze of friends and flattery.

Go hide thee quick in some deep wild,
    And carol as a brown thrush may.   10
Much petting spoils a gifted child.
    Go sing for us; go now, this day!

Tell how that Indian hunter died
    That wintry day between the hill
And frozen river; how he cried   15
    In vain for help, and how he still

Is heard on stormy nights to cry,
    And beat the wolves without avail;
And how his bones were left to dry
    And scatter in that lonely vale.   20

Photocopy of an undated newspaper clipping, box 1-22.6, Littlefield Collection, ANPA. Posey notes in his journal that he wrote this poem on March 9, 1897. An undated manuscript of this poem on Creek Orphan Asylum stationery is in folder 93 of the Gilcrease Posey Collection, and another identical manuscript version is housed in folder 140.

Line 2: A poet, teacher, and newspaper editor, George Riley Hall (1865–1944) was one of Posey's best friends. See Littlefield, *Alex Posey*, 71–72, 81–97, 137, 196.

Line 3: Tulledega is Posey's name for the rural area west of Eufaula, Muscogee (Creek) Nation, where he spent part of his childhood.

To Our Baby, Laughing [To Baby Yahola]

If I were dead, sweet one,
    So innocent,
I know you'd laugh the same
    In merriment,
And pat my pallid face   5
    With chubby hands and fair,
And think me living as
    You'd tangle up my hair.

If I were dead, loved one,
    So young and fair,   10
If I were laid beneath
    The grasses there,
My face would haunt you for
    A while—a day maybe—
And then you would forget,   15
    And not remember me.

Undated manuscript on Creek Orphan Asylum stationery, folder 79, Posey Collection, Gilcrease. A manuscript of this poem in folder 140 of the Gilcrease Posey Collection has an alternate title: "To Baby Yahola."

Line 1: This poem was written for Posey's first son, Yahola Irving Posey, who was born on March 29, 1897.

The Two Clouds

Away out West, one day,
Two clouds were seen astray.

One came up from the sea,
    Afar unto the South,
And drifted wearily.   5
    One came out of the North.

Away out West that day,
A town was swept away!

Photocopy of an undated clipping from the *Checotah Inquirer*, box 1-22.11, Littlefield Collection, ANPA. According to Posey's journal, he wrote this poem on April 6, 1897. Later that month, in his April 19, 1897, journal entry, he writes, "Send a poem to the Inquirer;" this poem was probably the one he mentions. A manuscript version of this poem, lacking stanza breaks, is in folder 140 of the Gilcrease Posey Collection.

The Rattler

Great heavens! Hold up! Don't you see
What you are riding onto there?
Quick! Jump down! Throw your reins to me!
(Whoa Bald) Don't give him any time
To sail, Shoot! There, he's done for now!   5
Gee Whiz, but isn't he rusty! Twice
Twelve rattles and a button! Whew!
Ram straws up in his nostrils. See,
They're four holes there as sure as fate!
If he were once to nip you on   10
The thigh, you'd cross the Great Divide
In just about as many steps!

Ledger, folder 140, Posey Collection, Gilcrease. Though an undated manuscript is the only source of this poem, it was probably written on April 27, 1897. On that day in his journal Posey mentions spending part of the day writing "a rattlesnake poem."

Line 9: Rattlesnakes possess pit-like organs located near each nostril.

June [Midsummer]

I see the millet combing gold
  From summer sun,
  In hussar caps, all day;
  And brown quails run
   Far down the dusty way,   5
Fly up and whistle from the wold;

Sweet delusions on the mountain,
  Of hounds in chase,
  Beguiling every care
  Of life apace,   10
  Though only fevered air
That trembles and dies in mounting.

Manuscript dated June 11, 1897, on Creek Orphan Asylum stationery, folder 82, Posey Collection, Gilcrease. In this manuscript the title "June" has been replaced with "Midsummer" in Minnie Posey's handwriting. Minnie incorporated this change into her 1910 edition, perhaps because there was another poem also called "June." In a later manuscript, which Minnie apparently did not consult, the poem is called "June" and lacks the final stanza. See folder 140, Posey Collection, Gilcrease.

The Idle Breeze

Like a truant boy, unmindful
Of the herd he keeps, thou, idle
Breeze, hast left the white clouds scattered
All about the sky and wandered
Down to play at leap frog with the   5
Grass and rest in the branches;
While, one by one, the white clouds stray
Apart and disappear forever.

Manuscript dated June 29, 1897, folder 83, Posey Collection, Gilcrease. The manuscript of "My Fancy" is also on this sheet.

My Fancy [Fancy]

Why do trees along the river
    Lean so far out o'er the tide?
Very wise men tell me why but
    I am never satisfied;
And so I keep my fancy still,   5
    That trees lean out to save
The drowning from the clutches of
    The cold, remorseless wave.

Manuscript dated June 29, 1897, folder 83, Posey Collection, Gilcrease. The manuscript of "The Idle Breeze" is also on this sheet. Another manuscript of this poem, simply entitled "Fancy," is housed in folder 140 of the Gilcrease Posey Collection. This alternate version has a third line that reads, "Cold reason tells one why but," and also includes a stanza break after the fourth line.

Autumn

In the dreamy silence
Of the afternoon, a
Cloth of gold is woven
Over wood and prairie;
And the jaybird, newly				5
Fallen from the heaven,
Scatters cordial greetings,
And the air is filled with
Scarlet leaves, that, dropping,
Rise again, as ever,				10
With a useless sigh for
Rest—and it is Autumn.

Manuscript dated October 20, 1897, on Creek Orphan Asylum stationery, folder 88, Posey Collection, Gilcrease. A manuscript of this poem bearing an alternate opening line that reads, "In the golden silence," is in folder 140 of the Gilcrease Posey Collection.

[Oh, to loiter where] [A Rhapsody]

Oh, to loiter where
    The sea breaks white
    In wild delight
    And throws her kisses evermore
    A slave unto the palm-set shore!   5

Oh, to wander where
    The gray moss clings,
    And south wind sings,
    Forever, low, enchantingly,
    Of islands girdled by the sea!   10

Oh, I'll journey back
    Some day; some day
    I'll go away;
    Forsake my land of mountain pine
    To win the heart that captured mine!   15

Manuscript dated November 7, 1897, on Creek Orphan Asylum stationery, folder 90, Posey Collection, Gilcrease. At the top of this manuscript, the title "A Rhapsody" has been written in Minnie Posey's handwriting.

To a Hummingbird

Now here, now there;
   E'er poised somewhere
In sensuous air.
  I only hear, I cannot see
The matchless wings that beareth thee.   5
   Art thou some frenzied poet's thought,
That God embodied and forgot?

Muskogee Phoenix, December 23, 1897. Manuscript dated July 3, 1897, folder 85, Posey Collection, Gilcrease. A manuscript of this poem is in folder 140 of the Gilcrease Posey Collection.

To the Century Plant

Thou art gloriously
Crowned at last with beauty;
And thy waxen blossoms,
Born of nameless patience,
Charm away the desert's 5
Dreariness, as some great
Truth a benefactor's
Cast in persecution
Sheds splendid glory
In another age.

Manuscript dated July 5, 1897, folder 84, Posey Collection, Gilcrease.

Line 2: The Century plant, or Mexican agave (*Agave americana*), flowers only after several years of maturation, after which it dies.

Verses Written at the Grave of McIntosh

O, carol, carol, early Thrush,
    A song
Where Oktahutche's water's rush
    Along!
In dewey bowers perched to greet 5
    The dawn,
Sing on, O songster ever sweet,
    Sing on!

And, list'ning to thy ecstasy,
    Oh, let me fancy that I hear, 10
    An echo of that voice so dear,
Thrown on the morning air by thee!

An echo of the voice
    Of McIntosh, my friend
And Indian brother, true, 15
    So true, unto the end.

    Carol, carol, sing,
    O bird of melody
    Say as sweet a thing
    Of him as he of thee! 20

    Blossom, blossom, swing
    Thy flowers lovingly,
    Sweet wild Rose of Spring,
    Here where his ashes lie!

As one by one the cold days pass, 25
    And Life and Love come on a-wing
      In early sens'ous days of Spring,
Creep gently hither, modest Grass,
Concealing every ugly cleft,
And cover up the wreck that's left 30
    By Winter rude and pitiless!
O April Beauty, then, come too,
In snow-white bonnet, sister true
    Of charity and tenderness
Ye oaks that spread broad branches at the Wind's behest 35
Be thou his monument, the watcher o'er his rest!

Twin Territories 3 (June 1901): 133. Manuscript dated August 10, 1897, folder 86, Posey Collection, Gilcrease. A manuscript bearing a fragment of this poem contains an alternate ending line that reads: "That lift up God's blue temple dome, guard ye his rest." This fragment is on a sheet torn from a ledger and housed in folder 140 of the Gilcrease Posey Collection. The poem's title refers to Daniel N. McIntosh (1822–1895), Muscogee statesman and Confederate colonel. See Debo, *Road to Disappearance*, 143–45.

Line 3: Oktahutche is the Muscogee name for the North Canadian River in eastern Oklahoma. Translated, the name means "Sand Creek."

To the Summer Cloud

Ever straying,
Never staying,
Never resting, e'er an aimless rover.
Did Shelley's spirit rise to thee,
Up from the cruel sea,   5
And dost thou bear it ever thro'
The vast unbounded blue,
Ever ranging,
Ever changing,
Ever yet the same the wide world over!   10

Manuscript dated September 7, 1897, on Creek Orphan Asylum stationery, folder 87, Posey Collection, Gilcrease. Another manuscript of this poem is in folder 140 of the Gilcrease Posey Collection.

Line 4: Percy Bysshe Shelley (1792–1822) was an English Romantic poet whose "Ode to the West Wind" and death by drowning Posey may be alluding to here.

To the Crow

Caw, caw, caw,
Thou bird of ebon hue,
Above the slumb'rous valley spread in flight,
On wings that flash defiance back at light,
A speck against the blue,   5
A-vanishing.

Caw, caw, caw,
Thou bird of common sense,
Far, far in lonely distance leaving me,
Eluded, with a shout of mockery   10
For all my diligence
At evening.

Manuscript dated October 27, 1897, on Creek Orphan Asylum stationery, folder 89, Posey Collection, Gilcrease.

To a Snowflake

This is no home for thee,
    Child of the winter cloud.
I question God why He,
    In blessing, has allowed

Thee to escape, unless   5
    It were to have thee bear
To Earth, in sinfulness,
    A sweet, white pardon there.

Twin Territories 1 (December 1899): 8. Manuscript dated December 13, 1897, on Superintendent of Public Instruction stationery, folder 91, Posey Collection, Gilcrease. The version of this poem found in the 1910 edition of Posey's poems removes the stanza break after line four.

Sea Shells

I picked up shells with ruby lips
    That spoke in whispers of the sea
Upon a time and watched the ships
    On white wings sail away in glee

The ships I saw go out that day   5
    Live misty dim in memory,
But still I hear, from far away,
    The blue waves breaking ceaselessly.

Muskogee Phoenix, December 23, 1897. A manuscript of this poem is in folder 140 of the Gilcrease Posey Collection.

The Bluebird

A winged bit of Indian sky
Strayed hither from its home on high.

Folder 137, Posey Collection, Gilcrease.

Coyote

A few days more and then
There'll be no secret glen,
Or hollow, deep and dim,
To hide or shelter him.

And on the prairie far,   5
Beneath the beacon star
On Evening's dark'ning shore,
I'll hear him nevermore.

For where the tepee smoke
Curled up of yore, the stroke   10
Of hammers ring all day,
And grim Doom shouts, "Make way!"

The immemorial hush
    Is broken by the rush
Of armed enemies   15
    Unto the utmost seas.

Folder 131, Posey Collection, Gilcrease. Another manuscript of this poem is in folder 140 and ends with these two lines: "Of man, his enemy, / Then to the utmost sea."

Distant Music

I hear a distant melody
    And years come crowding back to me,
Thro' vistas dim of memory,
    As ships to haven from the sea,

Each freighted with the dreams of youth,   5
    And moor them in the restless bay
About my heart awhile and then
    Each sail away—so far away

I fancy that I sit beside
    The shore of slumber's phantom sea,   10
Behold sweet visions die and hear
    The siren voices calling me.

Folder 129, Posey Collection, Gilcrease. See "Distant Music [early draft]" for an earlier version of this poem and for an explanation of how Minnie Posey altered that early draft in her 1910 edition of her husband's poems.

Distant Music [early draft]

I hear a distant melody,
    And years come crowding back to me,
Thro' vistas dim of memory,
    As ships to haven from the sea;

Each freighted with the dreams of youth,   5
    And moor them in the restless bay
About my heart a while and then
    Each sail away—so far away!

I fancy that I sit beside
    The shore of slumbers' phantom sea   10
And see sweet visions die and hear
    The siren voices calling me.

    I hear it ever;
    It ceases never;
    On land and sea   15
    It follows me,

So soft and low and far away,
    Like echoes dying in the folded hills.
I hear it here, go where I may,
    A cure for all the sad heart's ills.   20

Am I a shell cast on the shore
    Of Time's illimitable sea
To hear and whisper evermore
    The music of Eternity?

Folder 136 and 150, Posey Collection, Gilcrease. In her 1910 edition of her husband's poems, Minnie Posey divided this early draft of "Distant Music" into two poems, giving them titles of her own making: "Mother's Song" and "At the Siren's Call." Posey himself selected the first three stanzas of this draft for "Distant Music," and he even wrote a clean draft of the poem in its final form; see folder 129. In preparing her posthumous collection of Posey's poems, Minnie ignored his version of "Distant Music" (it does not appear in her edition) and divided the stanzas. Minnie made stanzas one, two, four, and five into "Mother's Song," and then placed stanzas three and six under the title of "At the Siren's Call." Minnie's reason for this alteration of her husband's poetry remains unknown. Perhaps she hoped to salvage Posey's abandoned stanzas, but her actions certainly violated her husband's authorial decisions.

Earth's Lilies and God's

Earth's starry lilies sink to rest,
    All folded in the mere at night
But God's slip back and slumber best,
    Sky-hidden, in the broad day light.

Folder 125, Posey Collection, Gilcrease; another manuscript of this poem is in folder 140.

Her Beauty

Her cheeks are garden spots
Of Touch-me-nots;
Her hair the gathered beams
Of sunny dreams;
And that her soul looks thro'   5
Are bits of fallen blue.

No wall hath circled yet,
Nor dews have wet,
A red rose like her lips.
Her finger-tips   10
They taper like a leaf;
Her heart is all mischief.

[She's God's improvement of
Her sex. O Love!
O Life! O Birds! O Light!   15
O Winds! O Night!
Ye are Heaven here
When she is near!]

Folder 133, Posey Collection, Gilcrease. The third stanza of this poem has been crossed out in the manuscript; it is included here in brackets. The first nine lines of "Her Beauty" were later incorporated into "A Valentine," possibly by Minnie Posey after her husband's death. See the source notes for "A Valentine" for more information.

[I sing but fragments]

I sing but fragments of
    A high born melody
Stray notes and castaways
    Of perfect harmony

Folder 138, Posey Collection, Gilcrease. Apparently Posey incorporated this fragment within the poem "[The Poet's Song]." The same manuscript page that has this fragment also contains the poem "A Picture."

Ingersoll

When love and the fireside inspired,
    Words dropped from his eloquent lips
Like music from the golden lyre
    Swept by Apollo's finger-tips.

Fort Gibson Post, October 15, 1904. Robert Green Ingersoll (1833–1899) was a lawyer and accomplished orator famous for his agnostic views. An undated manuscript version of this poem is in folder 124 of the Gilcrease Posey Collection. A canceled fragment found at the top of the same manuscript page and apparently meant for another poem reads:

> "I have wandered back thro' the mist of the years
> With what sad, heavy heart and eyes full of tears
> I have relived the days of my youth today
> Did I muse on the scenes so sacred for aye.
> I heard voices that speak nevermore   5
> Sing and laugh and talk as of yore."

Life's Mystery

I wander by the shore of life,
    Enchanted by the voices from the sea;
Forever trying—like a child—
    In vain, to understand its mystery.

Folder 139, Posey Collection, Gilcrease.

A Picture

Lo! what a vivid picture here
    Of sin and purity
Here where the rivers join their hands
    And journey to the sea

A dirty, earthly look hath one   5
Reflects not back the sky
But on the other's bosom rests
    The smiles of chastity.

Folder 138, Posey Collection, Gilcrease. The poem "Where the Rivers Meet" appears to be an alternate version of "A Picture." This alternate version is included in this edition. Also found on the manuscript of "A Picture" is an untitled stanza that begins with the line "[I sing but fragments of]," and a full transcription of this fragment is included in this edition.

Sequoyah

The ages will remember thee,
    Illustrious Indian, poets tell
Thy story. Thou'st a star to be;
    Aye, one whose light has not yet fell,
But which is shining far away 5
And cannot reach the world today.

Folder 127, Posey Collection, Gilcrease. Sequoyah (1770?–1843) invented the Cherokee syllabary.

To Wahilla Enhotulle (To the South Wind)

O Wind, hast thou a sigh
    Robbed from her lips divine
Upon this sunbright day—
    A token or a sign?

Oh, take me, Wind, into
    Thy confidence, and tell
Me, whispering soft and low,
    The secrets of the dell.

Oh, teach me what it is
    The meadow flowers say,
As to and fro they nod
    Thro' all the golden day.

Oh, hear, Wind of the South,
    And whispering softer yet,
Unfold the story of
    The pine tree's regret.

Oh, waft me echoes sweet
    That haunt the meadow glen,
The scent of new-mown hay
    And songs of harvest men.

The coolness from the sea
    And forests dark and deep,
The soft reed notes of Pan
    And bleat of straying sheep.

Oh, make me, Wind, to know 25
    The language of the bee,
The burden of the wild
    Bird's rapturous melody.

The pass-word of the leaves
    Upon the cottonwood; 30
And let me join them in
    Their mystic brotherhood.

Undated clipping, scrapbook, Posey Collection, Gilcrease. An undated manuscript of this poem is in folder 134.

Line 23: In Greek mythology Pan is the god of the forest and fertility who bears the feet, ears, and horns of a goat.

[Upon Love's sea, our barques shall sail]
[Drifting Apart]

Upon Love's sea, our barques shall sail
    No more together;
The dark'ning sky and rising gale
    Bring stormy weather.

The cruel Fates, at last, sweetheart,   5
    Our love must sever;
Must furl our sails, drift us apart
    For aye and ever.

I pray a sunny port be thine
    When storm is over   10
I know whatever lot be mine,
    I'm still thy lover.

Folder 132, Posey Collection, Gilcrease. The 1910 edition titles this poem "Drifting Apart," but there is no title on the manuscript.

What My Soul Would Be

What mountain glens afar
And woodland valleys are
To echoes in the air,
My soul would be
To harmony. 5

Folder 126, Posey Collection, Gilcrease.

In the Winter Hills

The sunshine, falling warm from
Out the low hung winter sky is
Dancing in the valleys; wreathes of
Haze, as blue as you can think, have
Circled all the hills; and birds, 5
Forgetting in their jubilance,
Are singing everywhere of Spring.
And, oh, to live! and, oh, to breathe
This Indian air and dream and dream
All day here in the winter hills! 10

Manuscript dated January 6, 1898, folder 95, Posey Collection, Gilcrease.

The Open Sky

   I look up at the open sky,
      And all the evils in
My heart the instant pale and die,
      For, lo! I cannot sin

Manuscript dated January 14, 1898, folder 96, Posey Collection, Gilcrease. The poem, "Sunset," is also on this manuscript page. Another manuscript of this poem is in folder 140.

Sunset

By coward clouds forgot,
    In yonder's sunset glow,
The day, in battle shot,
    Lies bleeding, weak, and low.

Manuscript dated January 14, 1898, folder 96, Posey Collection, Gilcrease. The poem "The Open Sky" is also found on this manuscript page. Another manuscript of this poem is in folder 140.

The Legend of the Red Rose

The red rose once was white
    As any flake of snow can be;
The sum of her delight
    Was knowledge of her purity—
        For so the pretty little legend goes.   5

But, on a luckless day,
    There bloomed outside the garden wall
A common wildwood flower,
    So wondrous sweet and fair and tall,
        That envy flushed the white cheeks of the Rose.   10

Manuscript dated February 15, folder 130, Posey Collection, Gilcrease. Though this manuscript does not include a year, Posey only worked as superintendent of public instruction for the Muscogee Nation from December 1897 to October 1898 (Littlefield, *Alex Posey*, 101). Assuming he only used this stationery during that time, he likely wrote this poem on February 15, 1898. The poem "My Pearl" also appears on this same manuscript page. The version of "The Legend of the Red Rose" that appears in the 1910 edition contains several variants that may originate in a revised version now lost, and reads:

    The red rose once was white
        As any flake of snow can be;
    The sum of her delight
        Was knowledge of her purity—
    As ev'ry Bee and nodding Poppy knows.   5
        But, in a luckless hour,
    There bloomed outside the garden wall
        A common wildwood flow'r,
    So wondrous fair and sweet and tall,
        That envy flushed the white face of the Rose!   10

My Pearl

I own a wee pink pearl,
    I picked up long ago,
Shaped like a falling tear
        On maiden cheeks aglow.

Manuscript dated February 18, folder 130, Posey Collection, Gilcrease. Assuming Posey only used this stationery during his time as superintendent of public instruction for the Muscogee Nation, he likely wrote this poem on February 18, 1898. The poem "The Legend of the Red Rose" also appears on this same manuscript page.

Brook Song

If you'll but pause and
    Listen, listen long,
There're far-off voices
    In a wee brook's song
That come as voices   5
    Come from out the years;
And you will dream you
    Hear the voice once *Her's*,
Perhaps, and wend on
    Blinded by your tears.   10

Manuscript dated March 27, 1898, folder 97, Posey Collection, Gilcrease. This poem is on the same page as "Prairies of the West."

Prairies of the West

Roll on, ye Prairies of the West,
    Roll on, like unsailed seas aways!
        I love thy silences
           And thy mysterious room.

Roll on, companions of my soul,   5
    Roll on, into the boundless day!

Manuscript dated March 27, 1898, folder 97, Posey Collection, Gilcrease. This poem is on the same page as "Brook Song." Posey incorporates all lines except the fifth into the later poem "The Homestead of Empire."

To Yahola, on His First Birthday

The sky has put her bluest garment on,
    And gently brushed the snowy clouds away;
The robin trills a sweeter melody,
    Because you are just one year old today.

The wind remembers, in his sweet refrains   5
    Away, away up in the tossing trees,
That you came in the world a year ago,
    And earth is filled with pleasant harmonies,

    And all things seem to say,
    "Just one year old today."   10

Manuscript dated March 28, 1898, folder 98, Posey Collection, Gilcrease. This poem was written for Posey's first son, Yahola Irving Posey, who was born on March 29, 1897.

To a Morning Warbler

Sing on till light and shadow meet,
    Blithe spirit of the morning air;
I do not know thy name, nor care;
    I only know thy name is sweet,
And that my heart beats thanks to thee,   5
Made purer by thy minstrelsy.

Fort Gibson Post, October 15, 1904; also published in *Indian's Friend*, April 1901, and *Muskogee Phoenix*, November 2, 1899. Manuscript dated March 31, 1898, folder 99, Posey Collection, Gilcrease.

Lowena

Blue hills between us lie
    And rivers broad and deep;
But here, as there, a bird
    Is singing me to sleep
And love has bridged the mountains blue 5
And all the streams between us two.

Kind friends they bid me stay
    And make their homes my own;
But they cannot be you
    To me and I'm alone 10
Amid the music sweet,
And shall be till we meet.

However kind the friends,
    The scenes however fair,
My heart returns to thee, 15
    Not happy anywhere
Save when thou art near to share
Life's light of joy or shade of care.

Manuscript dated May 31, 1898, folder 100, Posey Collection, Gilcrease. The title refers to Posey's pet name for his wife, Minnie Harris Posey (born on February 3, 1873). Minnie Posey explained in a letter to Edward Everett Dale that the name meant "loving the bright and happy." See Minnie H. Posey to Edward Everett Dale, February 19, 1919, Dale Collection, Western History Collection, University of Oklahoma, Norman.

[The Poet's Song]

The poet sings but fragments of
    A high-born melody.
A few stray notes and castaways
    Of perfect harmony
That come to him like murmurs from   5
    The sea of mystery.

Manuscript dated June 30, 1898, folder 101, Posey Collection, Gilcrease. The title of this poem is written in Minnie Posey's handwriting and probably derives from her. This poem appears to incorporate the fragment "[I sing but fragments of]," which is included in this edition. This manuscript also contains the poem "[We take no notice of]."

[We take no notice of]

We take no notice of
    The sunshine falling everywhere
Nor care for it until
    We see it only here and there.

Manuscript dated June 30, 1898, folder 101, Posey Collection, Gilcrease. This manuscript also contains the poem "The Poet's Song."

[Nature's Blessings]

Tis mine to be in love with life,
    And mine to hear the robins sing;
Tis mine to live apart from strife
    And kneel to flowers blossoming—
    To all things fair—　　　　　　　　　　　　5
        As at a shrine—
    To drink the air
        As I would wine.

To Love, I've built a temple here,
    Beneath the boughs of oak and pine,　　　10
Beside a spring that, all the year,
    Tells of a harmony divine.
    I own no creeds
        Sweet Love beside—
    My spirit's needs　　　　　　　　　　　　15
        Are satisfied.

For all the pleasures of the King,
    For all the joys the rich man feels,
For all the bliss that gold can bring,
    I would not turn upon my heels.　　　　20
    A hush, sunshine,
        A clamb'ring vine
    Upon the wall
        Is worth them all.

Manuscript dated July 1, 1898, folder 102, Posey Collection, Gilcrease. The title of this poem is written in Minnie Posey's hand and is probably her creation. The version of this poem found in the 1910 edition omits the third stanza and fails to indent the second and fourth lines.

Twilight [July 7, 1898]

O Twilight, fold me, let me rest within
    Thy dusky wings;
For I am weary, weary. Lull me with
    Thy whisperings,
So tender; let my sleep be fraught with dreams   5
    Of beauteous things.

Manuscript dated July 7, 1898, folder 103, Posey Collection, Gilcrease. The portion of the title in brackets differentiates it from another poem of the same title.

June [July 10, 1898]

A maid, of shape divine,
    Who holds, in ash to sup,
    An over brimming cup
Of sensuous sunshine.

Manuscript dated July 10, 1898, folder 104, Posey Collection, Gilcrease. The portion of the title in brackets differentiates it from another poem bearing the same title.

The West Wind [Husse Lotka Enhotulle]

From o'er the hills it comes to me,
    The clouds pursuing,
With song of bird and drone of bee,
    So soft and wooing;

From o'er the woods, thro' shade and sheen,   5
    With fragrance teeming,
From o'er the prairies, wide and green,
    And leaves me dreaming.

Across the fields of corn and wheat
    In valleys lying,   10
It seems to sing a message sweet
    Of peace undying.

I shout aloud—the wildwoods ring
    As they have never—
"Blow, O Wind of the West, and sing   15
    This song forever!"

Manuscript dated August 7, 1898, folder 105, Posey Collection, Gilcrease. According to marks on the manuscript, Posey later placed lines 9 and 10 before lines 11 and 12. The earlier version reversed this order. Posey's change has been retained in this edition. The title "Husse Lotka Enhotulle" is written in Minnie Posey's handwriting and is probably her own addition to the poem.

Morning

The cloud-dykes burst, and lo
    The Night is swept away
And drowned in overflow
    Of Light at break of day!

Manuscript dated August 11, 1898, folder 106, Posey Collection, Gilcrease.

The Athlete and the Philosopher

In Greece, an athlete boasted once
    That he could outswim anyone.
"So can a goose," remarked a sage,
    With eyes alive with wholesome fun.

The athlete boasted on, "And I 5
    Can deeper dive than any man."
"So can a bullfrog," said the sage.
    But, heedless still, the fool began,

"And more than that, can higher kick
    Than any living man in Greece." 10
"And so can any jackass," said
    The sage. The athlete held his peace.

Manuscript dated August 13, 1898, folder 107, Posey Collection, Gilcrease.

Eyes of Blue and Brown

Two eyes met mine
    Of heav'n's own blue—
Forget-me-nots
    Seen under dew;

My heart straightway   5
    Refused to woo
All other eyes
    Except those two.

Days came and went
    A whole year thro,   10
And still I loved
    Two eyes of blue.

But when one day
    Two eyes of brown,
In olive set   15
    Beneath a crown

Of browner hair,
    Met mine, behold,
The eyes beneath
    The shining gold,   20

Love-lit and loved
    In days of yore,
Grew dim, and were
    Sky-blue no more!

Manuscript dated August 21, 1898, folder 108, Posey Collection, Gilcrease.

Flowers

When flowers fade, why do
    Their fragrances linger still?
Have they a spirit, too,
    That Death can never kill?

Is it their Judgment Day												5
    When from the dark, dark mould
Of April and of May
    Their blooms again unfold?

Manuscript dated August 26, 1898, folder 109, Posey Collection, Gilcrease.

Mount Shasta

Behold, the somber pines have pitched their tents
    At Shasta's base like hosts of Night;
For aye besieging in his battlements—
    For aye in vain—their monarch, Light!

Though seas dry up and empty deserts bloom;   5
    Though races come and pass away
From earth, it still, it still is seen to loom
    And to flash back God's smile for aye!

Manuscript dated September 10, 1898, folder 110, Posey Collection, Gilcrease.

The Dew and the Bird

There is more glory in a drop of dew,
    That shineth only for an hour,
Than there is in the pomp of earth's great Kings
    Within the noonday of their pow'r.

There is more sweetness in a single strain   5
    That falleth from a wild bird's throat,
At random in the lonely forest's depths,
    Than there's in all the songs that bards e'er wrote.

Yet men, for aye, rememb'ring Caesar's name,
    Forget the glory in the dew,   10
And praising Homer's epic let the lark's
    Song fall unheeded from the blue.

Manuscript dated September 16, 1898, folder 111, Posey Collection, Gilcrease.

Line 9: Gaius Julius Caesar (100–44 BC), a Roman statesman who initiated the Roman imperial system, was assassinated by a group of senators who feared his popularity would make him a king.

The Deer

From out the folded hills,
    That lie beneath a thin blue veil,
There comes a deer to drink
    From Limbo's waters in the dale.

Then flies he back into   5
    The hills, and sitting here, I dream
And watch, as vain as he,
    My image lying in the stream.

Manuscript dated September 25, 1898, folder 112, Posey Collection, Gilcrease.

Line 4: Limbo Creek runs through the Tulledega Mountain area of Posey's childhood home.

Be It My Lot

Upon the rocks that frown
    Above the North Fork river,
Are couches green of moss,
    Where one could rest forever;
Cast all his cares aside
    And dream of troubles never.

Be it my lot someday,
    When life is gusty weather
And snow falls thick in June
    And all my roses wither,
To leave the cold world far
    Behind and journey thither.

Manuscript dated September 26, 1898, folder 113, Posey Collection, Gilcrease. The original title of this poem was "Be It My Lot Someday," but at some point Posey crossed out the last word in the title.

When Love Is Dead

Who last shall kiss the lips
    Of love when Love is dead?
Who last shall fold her hands
    And pillow soft her head?

Who last shall vigil keep   5
    Beside her lonely bier?
I ask, and from the dark
    Cold night without, I hear

The mystic answer: "I
    Her mother, Earth, shall press   10
Her lips the last in my
    Infinite tenderness."

Twin Territories 2 (October 1900): 35. Manuscript dated September 28, 1898, folder 114, Posey Collection, Gilcrease. The version of this poem found in the 1910 edition has lines arranged in a significantly different order. As the version presented here matches both the original manuscript and the version published during Posey's lifetime, it probably best reflects his wishes.

To the Morning Glory

The sun hath never set
    Upon thy beauty yet.
Long ere the noonday beams appear,
Thou diest in thy loveliness.

But wintry days await,   5
And trials sere and great,
Along the path that I must go
Ere withered youth finds rest below.

Manuscript dated October 2, 1898, folder 115, Posey Collection, Gilcrease.

To an Over-Stylish Miss

The jewels on your fingers fair
    Cannot increase your beauty, miss;
Nor all the costly silks you wear
    Add to the sweetness of your kiss.

Your teeth are pearls sufficient, miss,   5
    And silks enough your wondrous hair.
I fear you've never thought of this
    That you contrive to look so rare.

I'm sure that Nature sorrows, miss,
    To see you so unsatisfied;
To know you've not a tithe of bliss   10
    For all the pains that she has plied.

A twilight blush was on your face,
    A dawn of hair was on your head!
But they, alas, have given place
    To artificial show and fled!   15

Manuscript dated October 2, 1898, folder 116, Posey Collection, Gilcrease.

[Farewell, frail leaf]

Farewell, frail leaf, till
Spring sets free the rill
    And puts life in the bough
And a song in the bird.
    From thy mould, thou will rise,   5
Like a spark that is stirred,
    To thy home in the skies
    That are desolate now!

Manuscript dated October 17, 1898, folder 117, Posey Collection, Gilcrease.

The Sunshine of Life

The smile of a mother,
The smile of a father,
The smile of a brother,
The smile of a sister,
    The smile of a sweetheart,   5
When fondly you've kissed her,
    The moment ere you 'part,
The sweet smile of a wife,
    And the smile of a friend
    Who proves true to the end,   10
Is the sunshine of life.

Manuscript dated October 22, 1898, folder 118, Posey Collection, Gilcrease.

Gone

Gone! leaving all her bright
    Hopes scattered, shell-like, on
    The shore of life. Gone! gone!
Like a white dove in flight.

[There hangs the robe she wore   5
    In matchless harmony
    And perfect purity;
She needs it now no more.]

She's but a memory
    Of kind deeds and of   10
    A life that was all love.
How sweet her rest must be

Beneath the leaves that fall
    From Autumn branches bare
    To slumber with her there   15
In answer to her call!

Dated October 22, 1898, the manuscript for this poem has been torn into two halves that now form the contents of folders 128 (the first two stanzas) and 119 (the final two stanzas), Posey Collection, Gilcrease. Posey crossed out the second stanza, but it is retained here in brackets. As the manuscript appears to have been deliberately torn in half, it is uncertain whether he abandoned the work, intended only the first stanza to survive, or divided the poem into two different texts.

Kate and Lou

So wondrous fair are Kate and Lou,
And both return my love so true,
I cannot choose between the two.
And so the rolling years go by,
Nor ever halt to question why 5
I cannot bring myself to woo
Sweet Kate and not love fair Lou too.

So wondrous fair are Kate and Lou,
And both return my love so true,
I cannot choose between the two, 10
And so, as the swift years roll by,
Alike I'll love them till I die;
For I can't bring myself to woo
Fair Lou and not love sweet Kate too.

Manuscript dated November 28, 1898, folder 120, Posey Collection, Gilcrease.

My Hermitage

Between me and the noise of strife
    Are walls of mountains set with pine;
The dusty care-strewn paths of life
    Lead not to this retreat of mine.

I live with Echo and with Song,   5
    And Beauty leads me forth to see
Her temple's colonnades, and long
    Together do we love to be.

The mountains wall me in complete,
    And leave me but a bit of blue   10
Above. All year, the days are sweet—
    How sweet! And all the long nights thro'

I hear the river flowing by
    Along its sandy bars;
Behold, far in the midnight sky,   15
    An infinite of stars!

'Tis sweet, when all is still,
    When darkness gathers round,
To hear, from hill to hill,
    The far, the wandering sound.   20

The cedar and the pine
    Have pitched their tents with me.
What freedom vast is mine!
    What room of mystery!

And on the dreamy southern breeze,   25
　　That steals in like a laden bee
And sighs for rest among the trees,
　　Are far-blown bits of melody.

What afterglows the twilights hold,
　　The darkening skies along!   30
And O, what rose-like dawns unfold,
　　That smite the hills to song!

High in the solitude of air,
　　The gray hawk circles on and on,
Till, like a spirit soaring there,   35
　　His image pales and he is gone!

The Red Man 15 (February 1900): 2; also published in *Indian's Friend* 12 (May 1900): 1. Manuscript dated November 28, 1898, folder 121, Posey Collection, Gilcrease. The version of this poem found in the 1910 edition of Posey's poems reprints the poem in a significantly different order from any known version from Posey's lifetime. As the version presented here is the last known to have been published during Posey's lifetime, it probably best reflects his wishes.

Line 5: In Greek mythology, Echo is a nymph who is deprived of her ability to speak by Hera and must instead repeat the words of others.

What I Ask of Life

I ask no more of life than sunset's gold;
    A cottage hid in songbird's neighborhood,
    Where I may sing and do a little good
For love and pleasant memories when I'm old.

If life hath this in store for me—   5
    A spot where coarse souls enter not,
Or strife, I'm sure there cannot be
    On earth a fairer heaven sought.

Manuscript dated December 12, 1898, folder 122, Posey Collection, Gilcrease.

A Glimpse

A hurried glimpse is all I had of her,
    Beyond the Brazos and the Trinity;
'Twere best I saw no more of her lest I
    Had bowed to her as some divinity.

Ledger, folder 140, Posey Collection, Gilcrease. As Posey mentions the Brazos River in this poem, his inspiration probably came from a trip he took to Galveston, Texas, in June 1897. In his June 24, 1897, journal entry he writes of his trip: "The moss woods beyond the Brazos—how beautiful!"

The Boston Mountains

When God had finished making earth,
He found He had a residue
Of rocks, poor soil and scrubby oaks,
For which, plan as He might, He had
No use; and so, despairing, swept   5
Them all up here together, 'tween
Fort Smith and town of Fayetteville.

Photocopy of an undated clipping, Box 1-22.6, Littlefield Collection, ANPA. A manuscript of this poem is in folder 140 of the Gilcrease Posey Collection and it replaces the final two lines with a single line that reads: "The trash up here in one huge pile!"

Line 7: Fort Smith and Fayetteville are both towns located in western Arkansas.

By the River's Brink

The sky is blue, the day so fair,
    I sit here by the river's brink—
        The Oktahutche, deep and wide—
    And dream awhile—in fancy think,
        Long looking down into the tide   5
    That floweth on and on as blue,
    My soul is drifting thither, too;
Till lost in willow shadows there.

Ledger, folder 140, Posey Collection, Gilcrease.

Line 3: Oktahutche is the Muscogee name for the North Canadian River in eastern Oklahoma. Translated, the name means "Sand Creek."

By the Shore of Life

I wander by the shore of life
    Enchanted by the voices from the sea;
Forever trying, like a child,
    In vain to understand its mystery.

Ledger, folder 140, Posey Collection, Gilcrease.

Chinkings

Just like that white washed fence
That man with good, hard sense
    And polished ways;
Rub 'gainst him, close and tight,
You'll carry off some white   5
    That'll wear for days.

The longer that I live
I find true friends more rare;
He's like a flea these days;
Right sure, you think he is   10
To find he isn't there.

Say your say and be away,
For these are times demanding this of you;
Men can't listen to all day
What might be said in just a word or two.   15

Undated clipping, scrapbook, Posey Collection, Gilcrease. A manuscript of this poem is in folder 140 of the Gilcrease Posey Collection. In this manuscript the stanzas take the form of three individual poems named, respectively, "Contact," "True Friends," and "Briefly." The final three lines of "True Friends" (here, stanza two) read:

    You put your finger where,
    Right sure, you think they are
        To find they are not there.

A Common Failing

There is a faint and subtle curse
    Of high authority
    That makes us rather be
The speaker to the audience
Than auditor in all of us.   5
    It seems a foolish thing,
Yet we would have men follow us
    And each one be a king.

Ledger, folder 140, Posey Collection, Gilcrease.

A Fable

String this with the pearls of Aesop:
A sachem, once upon a time,
So say the prophets of the Creeks,
Convoked a mighty council,
Declared that he could learn no more,   5
And thereupon prepared to die.
But loath to leave this world without
Indulging in the luxury
Most dear to him—his usual smoke—
He asked his daughter for a coal   10
Of fire, wherewith to light his pipe.
She brought the coal on ashes in
Her palm, and up the sachem jumpt,
"What folly! Foolish man!" said he,
"I'm taught a lesson by a child!"   15

Undated clipping, scrapbook, Posey Collection, Gilcrease. A manuscript of this poem is in folder 140 of the Gilcrease Posey Collection.

Epigrams

Man is mortal and not divine,
Ruled by woman, made drunk by wine,
Loved of angels, by devils sought
His pride is vain—but God hath wrought!

Read the riddle—grace to the skies— 5
Are some born fools, are some born wise?
Tell me, Wizard, regarding man,
Why most men "can't" and yet some "can."

Why some with brains on certain line
Are yet absurd where others shine? 10
Are many free of these weak spots
Enough to laugh at harder lots?

God did decree this painful thing—
Humbled man's pride because of sin:
That all are fools, and all are wise— 15
But then he made us different eyes.

There are men wearing broadcloth who are not able to clothe their ideas well.

Some men will ask impossible things of you and then become your enemies.

When you ask a man for a favor, do not get mad at him if he requires you to give him your note.

Some individuals do not even pay the world rent for the room they take up in it.

Prosperity tends to impair the memory of some individuals who can remember readily when pinched for means.

When a man says the world is bad, let him show some proof that he has tried to make it better.

When a man throws his head backward and puts on a wise mysterious look, you are in no danger of being shot down by a new idea.

Those who wonder why Gen. Otis is not ousted from his command in the Philippines, fail to reflect that his pull with the administration is made of Manila hemp.

Many individuals dream of castles in pole pens; of magnificent estates on a ten-acre sofky patch, and of other impossibilities; but few, very few lay hold on the things within their reach.

When a man becomes so good that he is in nobody's way; when everybody is prompt to say but well of him. I tell you, sir, you can put it down, and safely too, that the world can move on without him.

When a man, who is not a frequent visitor, comes to your house, you can be certain that he has an ax to grind. And, as he will in his talk, prowl in the neighborhood of his wants, you can soon acquaint yourself with his motive without inviting him to tell you about it.

Undated clipping, scrapbook, Posey Collection, Gilcrease. A manuscript of two of the epigrams found in this later published version is in folder 140 of the Gilcrease Posey Collection. In that manuscript, stanzas ten and fourteen take the form of individual poems titled, respectively, "Be Fair" and "Goodness."

Line 31: Elwell Stephen Otis (1838–1909) was the unpopular commanding general of the forces in the Philippines during the Philippine-American War. In 1878 he published a book entitled *The Indian Question*, which contained chapters such as "Can the Indian Be Civilized?" and "How Can the Indian be Controlled and Improved?" Posey's animosity for Otis probably stems from his reading of this book.

Line 35: Sofky (variously spelled "sofky," "sofki," "sofke," or "sofkee") is a traditional Muscogee food made by cooking corn in lye water. See Wright, *Creeks and Seminoles*, 21, and Iness et al., *Beginning Creek*, 189.

God and the Flying Squirrel (A Creek Legend)

"I'm pleased with thee;
Go climb a tree,"
Said God, when He had made
Thy Flying Squirrel. "Nay,"
Replied the creature, half afraid,   5
"I want to fly away."

"You anger me;
Go climb a tree!"
Spoke God, in wrath, But still
The creature longed to fly.   10
"Alas! You treat me ill,"
It weeping gave reply.

When God into
A passion flew
And stretched the rascal's skin   15
Right roughly from his sides
And threw him high up in
The branches, where he hides.

Ledger, folder 140, Posey Collection, Gilcrease.

In Tulledega

Where mountains lift their heads
    To clouds that nestle low;
Where constant beauty spreads
    Sublimer scenes below;

Where gray and massive rocks   5
    O'erhang rough heights sublime;
Where awful grandeur mocks
    The brush, and poet's rhyme,

We saw the ev'ning blush
    Above the rugged range,   10
We heard the river rush
    Far off and faint and strange.

Undated clipping, scrapbook, Posey Collection, Gilcrease. A manuscript of this poem is in folder 140 of the Gilcrease Posey Collection. Tulledega is Posey's name for the rural area west of Eufaula, Muscogee (Creek) Nation, where he spent part of his childhood.

In Vain

Blow! O Wind of the sea!
O, blow! until I see
The ship that went away
Sail safe into the bay!

Wind of the sea! Wind of the sea! 5
What tidings dost thou bring to me?

But there's no reply;
There's no sail in sight;
And the years go by
And her hair grows white. 10

Ledger, folder 140, Posey Collection, Gilcrease.

The Inexpressible Thought

'Tis said that Moses only saw
    The radiance of Deity;
'Tis so we see the thought that we
    Can never utter perfectly.

Ledger, folder 140, Posey Collection, Gilcrease.

July

The air without has taken fever,
Fast I feel the beating of its pulse;
The leaves are twisted on the maple,
In the corn the autumn's premature;
The weary butterfly hangs waiting
For a breath to waft him thither at
The touch; the grass is curled and dust-blown;
The sun shines down as on a desert.

The air without is blinding dusty;
Cool I feel the west wind; I see
The sunlight, crowded on the porch, grow
Smaller till absorbed in shadow; the
Far hills erstwhile blue are changed to a gray;
Twilight shadows all the land apace;
And now I hear the shower falling
And the leaves clapping their hands for joy.

Ledger, folder 140, Posey Collection, Gilcrease. A variant of this poem appeared in the 1910 edition. See *The Poems of Alexander Lawrence Posey*, comp. Minnie H. Posey (Topeka: Crane, 1910), 106. There is no copy of this version dating from Alexander Posey's lifetime, and as Minnie Posey sometimes altered her husband's work, this 1910 version may not reflect his wishes. This later version matches the previous one until line seven, after which it reads:

> The touch, but falls, like truth unheeded,
> Into dust-blown grass and hollyhocks.
>
> The air without is blinding dusty;
> Cool I feel the breezes blow; I see   10
> The sunlight, crowded on the porch, grow
> Smaller till absorbed in shadow; and
> The far blue hills are changed to a gray, and
> Twilight lingers in the woods between;
> And now I hear the shower dancing   15
> In the cornfield and the thirsty grass.

The Man-Catcher

The man who can ensnare,
    By trick and fond caress,
Another unaware,
    May not at all possess
The smooth ability 5
To catch and kill a flea.

Undated clipping, scrapbook, Posey Collection, Gilcrease. A manuscript of this poem is in folder 140 of the Gilcrease Posey Collection and has an alternate ending line that reads: "To catch an active flea."

Meaningless

Till baby lips have spoken "papa, mamma,"
    There is no meaning in the words at all;
The house is but a pile of brick or lumber
    Till baby feet have pattered thro' the hall.

Ledger, folder 140, Posey Collection, Gilcrease.

The Milky Way

A fast path winding thro'
The vast star-sprinkled blue
And ending at the gate
Where God's white angels wait.

Ledger, folder 140, Posey Collection, Gilcrease.

Miser

O miser, why art thou a miser, pray?
Was Nature very stingy with your clay?

Ledger, folder 140, Posey Collection, Gilcrease.

A Vision of June [Narcissus—A Sonnet]

At last, my white narcissus is in bloom;
    Each blossom breathes a wondrous fragrance. Lo!
From over bleak December's waste of snow,
In summer garments, lightly thro' the gloom,
    Comes June to claim the truant in my room   5
    With her, the airs of sunny meadows come,
    And in the apple boughs I hear the hum
Of bees; in all the valleys, brooks resume,
'Twixt greening banks, their murmurous melody,
    The sunlight bursts in splendor in the blue,   10
And soon the narrow walls confining me,
    Recede into the distance from my view;
My spirit in the Summer's largeness grows,
And every thorn is hidden by the rose.

The *Philadelphia Press*, November 4, 1900. See clipping, scrapbook, Posey Collection, Gilcrease. An undated manuscript of this poem is in folder 158 of the Gilcrease Posey Collection. This manuscript page also contains a version of the poem, "All the While [Let Men Dispute.]" The poem immediately following this one, "Narcissus—A Sonnet," originates from a revised manuscript in a ledger circa 1899 (folder 140 Gilcrease Posey Collection). As these two versions allow a glimpse of Posey's creative process, both are provided in this edition.

Narcissus—A Sonnet

At last, my white Narcissus is in bloom,
    And breathes a wondrous fragrance forth; and, lo,
    Far over bleak December's waste of snow,
Like some supernal maiden lost in gloom,
Comes June to claim the truant in my room,   5
    With her, the winds from verdant meadows come
    And in the apple boughs I hear the hum
of bees and in the valleys brooks resume
elate their tardy journey to the sea.
    The sunlight bursts in splendor in the blue   10
And swift the narrow walls confining me
    [Exude] into the distance from my view,
From Winter's burrow a [indecipherable] and sombre skies.
I am transported into paradise.

Ledger, folder 140, Posey Collection, Gilcrease. With the exception of the title, Posey crossed out this entire poem. For more information, see the endnote for "A Vision of June [Narcissus—A Sonnet]."

Not Love Always

'Tis not love in every instance
    That makes one trust another kind;
'Tis often prompted by the fear
    Of daggers in the dark behind.

Ledger, folder 140, Posey Collection, Gilcrease.

On Piney

Far away from the valley below,
Like the roar in a shell of the sea,
Or the flow of the river at night
Comes the voice strangely sweet of the pines.
Snowy clouds, sometimes white, sometimes dark,   5
Like the joys and the sorrows of life,
Sail above, half becalmed in the blue;
And their cool shadows lie on the hills.

Here and there, when the leaves blow apart,
To admit sunny winds seeking rest   10
In the shade with their burthen of sweets,
Piney Creek shimmers bright, with a cloud

Or a patch of the sky on its breast;
Here the din and the strife of the mart
And the gabble of lips that profane,   15
Are heard not, and the heart is made pure.

Undated clipping, scrapbook, Posey Collection, Gilcrease. A manuscript of this poem is in folder 140 of the Gilcrease Posey Collection. That manuscript, entitled "On the Piney," includes a stanza break after the fourth line. This difference may indicate that the missing stanza break and perhaps even the title change in "On Piney" are printer's errors.

Our Deeds [A Simile]

Like bits of broken glass
Chance scatters in the sun,
Our deeds reflect the light
We carry in the world.

Ledger, folder 140, Posey Collection, Gilcrease. The version of this poem in the 1910 edition is titled "A Simile."

Pedantry

Some men are like some broad,
    Broad rivers that I know,
That flow majestically,
    Look deep, but are not so.

Ledger, folder 140, Posey Collection, Gilcrease.

Say Something

Form something when you'd have men heed;
Don't bark when you have nothing treed.

Ledger, folder 140, Posey Collection, Gilcrease.

September

A distant hill asleep in light blue haze
    And soft—a Moorish lady in her veils—
    And ev'rywhere reunions of the quails
And early morning hints of cooler days.

Undated clipping, scrapbook, Posey Collection, Gilcrease. A manuscript of this poem is in folder 140 of the Gilcrease Posey Collection.

A Thin Quilt's Warmth

There is warmth 'neath a quilt that is thin
    And a sleep that is perfect and sound;
And the secret is simple as sin:
    Just keep still and do not move around.
To be brief, straighten out, as if dead,   5
Covered up from your feet to your head.

Ledger, folder 140, Posey Collection, Gilcrease.

Thoughts

People either get more or less than their deserts.

When a man does his duty, he's got a job.

However fate may conspire against a man he still has something to be thankful for.

Ledger, folder 140, Posey Collection, Gilcrease.

To a Common Flower

1 Thy waxen blooms of yesterday
2 Today all wither and decay.
3 But, oh, so sweet a life is thine!
    5 Never knowing ill words spoken,
      6 Sorrows of a heart that's broken,   5
4 So full of days unlike to mine.

Ledger, folder 140, Posey Collection, Gilcrease. The numbers Posey wrote at the beginning of the lines most likely indicate a change in the arrangement of the poem. As the numbers provide insight into Posey's creative process, the poem is presented as found.

To a Face Above the Surf

To steal sweet kisses from thy brow,
    A lightsome zephyr I would be;
A brook to murmur thee a vow
    Of love and constancy.

To feel thy fingers' soft caress,   5
    A wayside flower I would be;
A grass blade for thy foot to press
    Upon the April lea.

Upon thy bosom fair to rest,
    A little sunbeam I would be;   10
A songster in the green forest
    To charm thee with my melody.

To clasp thee in a wild embrace;
    To press thy pink lips rapturously;
To look upon thee face to face,   15
    I would that I could be the sea!

Ledger, folder 140, Posey Collection, Gilcrease. The first stanza of "To a Face Above the Surf" was later incorporated into "A Valentine," perhaps by Minnie Posey while she was collecting works for her 1910 edition of her husband's poems. Posey, or possibly Minnie, crossed out this poem in the manuscript. See the source notes for "A Valentine" for more information.

To a Winter Songster

Sweet, sweet, sweet is the song you sing,
    Bonny bird, on the leafless tree;
And tender are the thoughts you bring
    To me as your own melody.
Sing on! I am sure, somewhere, May 5
And Love are lingering on the way.

Ledger, folder 140, Posey Collection, Gilcrease.

To Hall

I ne'er could selfish be—
    P'raps that's why I'm threadbare!
Good wine is naught to me
    Unless some friend can share.

So when your verses came—
    And better I ne'er read,
Tho' bearing Byron's name—
    I felt it in my head

I had received a jug
    Of Bourbon labeled "old"—
No peddler's juice of bug
    At Indian councils sold!

And when I did apprise
    Friend Grayson of the fact,
He opened wide his eyes
    And said, "Is it intact?"

"It is," was my reply,
    "Come, let us drink." He came.
He took some on the sly
    And gave your bourbon fame.

He took some more and more
    And by the Great Horn Spoon,
He tumbled on the floor
    Dead tipsy pretty soon!

John Thornton passing by 25
   To make some dunning call,
Our bourbon did espy
   And yanked it, jug and all!

Thief! I could smash his crown
   Like a dark alley thug 30
He made himself and town
   Drunk with the stolen jug!

Ledger, folder 140, Posey Collection, Gilcrease. A poet, teacher, and newspaper editor, George Riley Hall (1865–1944) was one of Posey's best friends. See Littlefield, *Alex Posey*, 71–72, 81–97, 137, 196.

Line 7: Byron (1788–1824), English romantic poet.
Line 11: A term for illegal whiskey.
Line 14: George W. Grayson (1843–1920) was one of Posey's best friends and was also an important Muscogee (Creek) political figure. He served as principal chief of the Muscogees from 1918 to 1920.
Line 25: John R. Thornton was the editor of the *Indian Journal* and together with Posey, Hall, and Grayson, served as a member of what the men termed "The Informal Club." According to Daniel F. Littlefield Jr., Thornton's "dunning call" was his attempt to collect newspaper subscriptions owed him by Posey and Grayson. Littlefield states that during this visit Thornton and Grayson read a poem Hall had sent to Posey. They compared the poem to good whiskey and Thornton decided to publish Hall's poem, without permission, in the *Indian Journal*. Posey's poem is meant as a lighthearted apology to Hall for publishing his poem without permission. An early draft of this poem was subtitled "An Apology for the Publication of a Poetic Epistle." See manuscript, "To George Riley Hall," Frederick S. Barde Collection, Archives and Manuscripts Division, Oklahoma Historical Society.

To Jim Parkinson

Thou art a frozen hearted man,
    Jim Parkinson,
And cold warts thy finger-tips
Thou snappest like a loggerhead,
    Jim Parkinson, 5
Kind words were never on thy lips.

Thou art a very stingy man,
    Jim Parkinson,
And very poor in charity.
Thou growlest like a fierce bulldog, 10
    Jim Parkinson,
At all the forms of poverty.

There was a man that died one time,
    Jim Parkinson,
And thou didst scoff his widow out 15
Imploring credit for a shroud,
    Jim Parkinson,
Her tearful pleading heeding not.

Thou hast a well of water fine,
    Jim Parkinson, 20
But thou art stingy, too, with that,
For thou hast taken off the pails,
    Jim Parkinson,
Now, move the well from where 'tis at!

Ledger, folder 140, Posey Collection, Gilcrease. Jim Parkinson is unidentified.

Line 4: Loggerhead, another name for a snapping turtle.

Trysting [Then and Now]

I laid amid the hum of bumble bees,
    And O, and O,
        Above me, to and fro,
The clover-heads were tossing in the breeze.

And O, and O, how cool their shadows lay   5
    Upon the lea,
        In dark embroidery!
How sweet the mock-bird sang, O perfect day!

The heavens in the south hung low and blue;
    Too low and blue   10
        For clouds to wander thro;
And so they moored at rest as white ships do.

My heart gave answer, bird, for thee and me
    O perfect day!
        For she is on her way   15
I know to join me in my reverie

Between that time and now, lie many years;
    And oh, and oh,
        And oh, time changes so!
The spring and summer wane and autumn seres.   20

Sing, Mockingbird upon the bending bough!
    Sing as of yore;
        My heart responds no more;
She listens, O, to sweeter music now.

Typescript of an undated newspaper clipping, Daniel F. Littlefield Jr. Collection, American Native Press Archives, University of Arkansas at Little Rock. A manuscript version of this poem, entitled "Then and Now and written in what appears to be Minnie Posey's handwriting, is in folder 140 of the Gilcrease Posey Collection. This manuscript version reverses the order of stanzas two and three.

Tulledega

My choice of all choice spots in Indian lands!
Hedged in, shut up by walls of purple hills,
That swell clear cut against our sunset sky,
Hedged in, shut up and hidden from the world.
As though it said, "I have no words for you;
I'm not a part of you; your ways aren't mine."
Hedged in, shut up with low log cabins built—
How snugly!—in the quaint old fashioned way;
With fields of yellow maize, so small that you
Might hide them with your palm while gazing on
Them from the hills around them, high and blue.
Hedged in, shut up with long forgotten ways,
And stories handed down from sire to son.
Hedged in, shut up with broad Oktaha, like
A flash of glory curled among the hills!
How it sweeps away toward the morning,
Deepened here and yonder by the beetling
Crag, the music of its dashings mingling
With the screams of eagles whirling over,
With its splendid tribute to the ocean!
And this spot, this nook is Tulledega;
Hedged in, shut up, I say, by walls of hills,
Like tents stretched on the borders of the day,
As blue as yonder op'ning in the clouds!

Undated clipping, scrapbook, Posey Collection, Gilcrease. A manuscript of this poem is in folder 140 of the Gilcrease Posey Collection. Tulledega is Posey's name for the rural area west of Eufaula, Muscogee (Creek) Nation, where he spent part of his childhood.

Line 14: A town in what is now Muskogee County in eastern Oklahoma.

A Vision

    In pensive mood she stood,
        In garments white like snow,
Beside the darksome wood,
        Amid the twilight glow;
As if she held communion there   5
    With spirits in the fading air.

    And loath to break the spell—
        The sweet enchantment that
She seemed to love so well,
        I back-ward stept, thereat   10
The beauteous vision fled from me
    In strange and silent mystery.

Ledger, folder 140, Posey Collection, Gilcrease.

What Profit

What profit is there in conversing, pray,
With him who nods assent to all you say?

Ledger, folder 140, Posey Collection, Gilcrease.

When Molly Blows the Dinner-Horn

'Tis twelve o'clock in Possum Flat;
The cabbage steams, and bacon's fat;
The bread is made of last year's corn—
When Molly blows the dinner-horn.

The shadows lengthen north and south; 5
The water wells up in your mouth;
You're neither sober nor forlorn,
When Molly blows the dinner-horn.

A quiet falls, the smoke curls up
Like incense from a censor cup; 10
It makes you glad that you were born.
When Molly blows the dinner-horn.

The cur, erstwhile stretched in a snore,
Lays stout siege to the kitchen door;
Nor will he raise it or be gone, 15
When Molly blows the dinner-horn.

Ledger, folder 140, Posey Collection, Gilcrease.

Line 1: This is Posey's ranch near Bald Hill. See Littlefield, *Alex Posey*, 96.

The Arkansas River

I dread thee, mighty River! There's a flush
Of anger on thy face that will not pale.
Thou'st treach'rous, turbulent, and move
Within thy roomy bed as if unconfined.
Before thy deep cold tide, and majesty,   5
Man pauses, lingers, and is mute with awe.
The white dust hanging over thee, when winds
Are high, must surely be the anxious ghosts
Of all the drowned, expecting that thou wilt
Someday go dry, and disappear from Earth.   10

Undated manuscript on Eufaula High School stationery, folder 146, Posey Collection, Gilcrease.

Assured

Be it dark; be it bright;
Be it pain; be it rest;
Be it wrong; be it right,
It must be for the best.

Some good must somewhere wait,   5
  And sometimes joy and pain
Must cease to alternate,
  Or else we live in vain.

Undated manuscript on Eufaula High School stationery, folder 151, Posey Collection, Gilcrease.

Lovingly [The Call of the Wild]

I'm tired of the gloom
In a four-walled room;
Heart-weary, I sigh
For the open sky
And the solitude 5
Of the greening wood,
Where the blue birds call
And the sunbeams fall
And the daisies lure
The soul to be pure. 10

I'm tired of the life
In the ways of strife;
Heart-weary, I long
For the river's song,
And the murmur of rills 15
In the breezy hills,
Where the pipe of Pan—
The hairy half-man—
The bright silence breaks
By the sleeping lakes. 20

Twin Territories 3 (March 1901): 47. The author of this poem is printed as "Chinnubbie Hays," which is probably a misreading of Posey's "Chinnubbie Harjo" signature. The poem is undoubtedly Posey's, and an earlier undated manuscript version titled "The Call of the Wild" on Eufaula High School stationery, is in folder 148 of the Gilcrease Posey Collection.

Line 17: In Greek mythology Pan is the god of the forest and fertility who bears the feet, ears, and horns of a goat.

Limbo [Esapahutche]

Now complaining and cross,
Through the reeds and the moss,
I come down with a roar,
To the green fields before,
From the hills of the old Dowdy Ranch—
From the valleys of pine where I branch—
From the hollows and coves where I lie
In the shade of the precipice high
Through the days of the unclouded sky.
And I flow,
As I go
Thro' the hills,
Into rills—
Into many a pool,
Overshadowed and cool;
Where the bright
    Lily's bloom
To a light
    In the gloom.
And I murmur all day,
    Impatient of delay,
        Ere I glide
            In the tide
                Of the wide
                    River, at
                        Cedar Flat.

Undated manuscript on Eufaula High School stationery, folders 152 and 153, Posey Collection, Gilcrease. The 1910 edition contains a poem titled "Ensapahutche (Gar Creek)" that appears to be a later revision of "Limbo." This 1910 version matches the previous one until line sixteen, at which it ends:

> Where the white lily-bloom
> Is a light in the gloom.
>
> Down the slope of the wild mountain-side
> Come the grasses athirst to my tide,
> By the Cardinal led aright.   20
> Far away, like the roar in the shell of the sea,
> The sad voice of the pine on the crag answers me,
> As I fall on the rocks at night.

Another similar manuscript version of this poem—lacking both a title and a date—can be found in folder 161 of the Posey Collection at the Gilcrease. Limbo refers to a creek near Posey's childhood home, and Gar Creek is also found in that area. The manuscript version of "Limbo" has the Muscogee word for Gar Creek, "Esapahutche," written in pencil across the top in Minnie Posey's handwriting, and this title may be her own creation. Furthermore, the 1910 edition uses the Seminole dialect variant for Gar Creek, "Ensapahutche." The Muscogee language has a number of dialects, and encountering different spellings and pronunciations in Indian Territory was not uncommon. Still, the reason for this difference remains unclear. For more information about the Muscogee words for "gar" and "creek" see Loughridge, *English and Muskokee Dictionary*, 129 and 150, and Martin and Mauldin, *Dictionary of Creek*, 31 and 57. Note the similarities of this poem with "[By the cardinal led aright]," "[Every moment I flow]" and "On Piney."

Line 5: Dowdy Ranch, which Posey also sometimes spelled as "Doughty," "Dawdy," and "Dowdie," is unidentified.

Line 26: Cedar Flat, an unidentified area apparently located in the vicinity of Posey's childhood Tulledega home.

[Every moment I flow]

Every moment I flow,
Willows ask me in vain:
Wither, O, do you go?
    Will you come back again?
I slip out of their arms—   5
    Long and beautiful though—
And away from their charms,
O whither, whither whither?
Birds chirp in pleasant weather.
But hither, hither, hither!   10
Forever and forever,
Far calls the distant river.
It's a long weary way
From the hills of the old Dawdy Ranch,
And the valleys of pine where I branch.   15

Undated manuscript on Eufaula High School stationery, folder 144, Posey Collection, Gilcrease. Note the similarities of this poem with "[By the cardinal led aright]," "Esapahutche [Limbo]" and "On Piney."

Line 14: Dawdy Ranch, which Posey also sometimes spelled as "Doughty," "Dowdy," and "Dowdie," is unidentified.

Memories

(Inscribed to my poet friend George Riley Hall)

What sweet and tender memories,
    What joys and griefs are yours and mine!
Hands rest that smote the ivory keys
    And still, the lips that sang, divine.
O'er lips that cannot say;   5
    O'er hearts that cannot beat,
The sky bends blue to-day,
    And flowers blossom sweet.

Dear ones, near ones have wended
    Homeward thro' the vale of tears;   10
The voice that charmed has blended
    With the silence of the years.

Though far apart we've drifted, Hall,
    'Tween you and me there's but a single river
And but a single mountain wall—   15
    'Tween Rose and Jim and us, the vast Forever!

The Press, November 4, 1900. See, clipping, scrapbook, Posey Collection, Gilcrease. Undated manuscript on Eufaula High School stationery, folder 149, Posey Collection, Gilcrease. Another manuscript version of this poem, lacking lines 5–8 and the fourth stanza, is in folder 140 of the Gilcrease Posey Collection. A poet, teacher, and newspaper editor, George Riley Hall (1865–1944) was one of Posey's best friends. See Littlefield, *Alex Posey*, 71–72, 81–97, 137, 196.

Line 16: Rosa "Rose" Lee was a good friend of Posey and worked as one of the teachers at the Creek Orphan Asylum during his tenure there. See Littlefield, *Alex Posey*, 91, 112–13, and 118. The deaths of Rosa Lee and Posey's brother, James Posey, served as inspiration for this poem.

The Mocking Bird

Whether spread in flight,
    Or perched upon the swinging bough,
Whether day or night,
    He sings as he is singing now—
Till every leaf upon the tree   5
Seems dripping with his melody!

    Hear him! hear him!
        As up he springeth—
        As high he wingeth
    From roof or limb!   10

    If you are sad,
        Go cry it out!
    If you are glad,
        Go laugh and shout!

Hear him! What heart can shut him out?   15
    He hath a song for every mood,
    For every song an interlude,
To dry the tear or stem the shout!

Whether you work, whether you rest,
    Hark! listen! hear him sing   20
As careless as he builds the nest
    For his mate in the spring!

Undated clipping, scrapbook, Posey Collection, Gilcrease. The manuscript of this poem is on Eufaula High School stationery, folder 142, Posey Collection, Gilcrease.

Spring in Tulwa Thlocco

Thro' the vine-embowered portal blows
    The fragrant breath of Summer time;
Far, the river, brightly winding, goes
    With murmurs falling into rhyme.

It is Spring in Tulwa Thlocco now,   5
    The fresher hue of grass and tree
All but hides upon the mountain's brow
    The green haunts of the chickadee.

There are drifts of plum blooms, snowy white,
    Along the lane and greening hedge;   10
And the dogwood blossoms cast a light
    Upon the forest's dusky edge.

Crocus, earliest flower of the year,
    Hangs out its starry petals where
The spring beauties in their hiding peer,   15
    And red buds crimson all the air.

Undated manuscript on Eufaula High School stationery, folder 150, Posey Collection, Gilcrease. Tulwa Thlocco is Muscogee (Creek) for "big town."

Where the Rivers Meet

Lo! what a vivid picture here
    Of sin and purity—
Here where the rivers join their
    Hands and journey to the sea!

A dirty, earthly look has one,   5
    Reflects not back the sky;
But mark how on the other's tide
    The clouds are passing by!

Twin Territories 3 (February 1901): 24. An undated manuscript version of this poem on Eufaula High School stationery is in folder 143 of the Gilcrease Posey Collection. This appears to be an alternate version of the poem "A Picture."

Ode to Sequoyah

The names of Watie and Boudinot—
    The valiant warrior and gifted sage—
And other Cherokees, may be forgot,
    But thy name shall descend every age;
The mysteries enshrouding Cadmus' name   5
Cannot obscure thy claim to fame.

The people's language cannot perish—nay,
    When from the face of this great continent
Inevitable doom hath swept away
    The last memorial—the last fragment   10
Of tribes,—some scholar learned shall pore
Upon they letters, seeking ancient lore.

Some bard shall lift a voice in praise of thee,
    In moving numbers tell the world how men
Scoffed thee, hissed thee, charged with lunacy!   15
    And who could not give 'nough honor when
At length, in spite of jeers, of want and need,
Thy genius shaped a dream into a deed.

By cloud-capped summit in the boundless west,
    Or mighty river rolling to the sea,   20
Where'er thy footsteps led thee on that quest,
    Unknown, rest thee, illustrious Cherokee!

Twin Territories 1 (April 1899): 102. Sequoyah (1776?-1843) invented the Cherokee syllabary.

Line 1: Stand Watie (1806–1871) was a Cherokee statesman and Confederate brigadier general. Born as Gallegina Watie, Elias Boudinot (c. 1802–1839) was a Cherokee statesman and the progressive editor of the *Cherokee Phoenix*.

Line 5: In Greek mythology Cadmus was a Phoenician prince who invented the Grecian alphabet.

Nightfall [Twilight]

As evening splendors fade
   From yonder sky afar,
The Night pins on her dark
   Robe with a large bright star,
And the new moon hangs like   5
   A high-thrown scimitar.
Vague in the mystic room
   This side the paling west,
The Tulledegas loom
   In an eternal rest,   10
And one by one the lamps are lit
   In the dome of the Infinite.

Twin Territories 4 (May 1902): 124. This poem, titled "Twilight," was also published in the November 4, 1900, issue of the *Philadelphia Press* and the November 26, 1899, issue of the *St. Louis Republic*. See undated clipping, scrapbook, Posey Collection, Gilcrease. Another version of this poem, titled "Nightfall" and bearing slight variations, was published in *Muskogee Phoenix*, November 2, 1899.

Line 9: The Tulledegas is Posey's name for the rural area west of Eufaula, Muscogee (Creek) Nation, where he spent part of his childhood.

An Outcast

Pursued across the waning year,
By winds that chase with lifted spear,
A leaf, blood-stained, fell spent at last
Upon my bosom. Poor Outcast!

Sturm's Oklahoma Magazine 1 (October 1905): 84. In Posey's lifetime this poem also appeared in the following publications: *Fort Gibson Post*, October 15, 1904; *Twin Territories* 4 (November 1902); *Twin Territories* 4 (May 1902); and *Muskogee Phoenix*, November 2, 1899.

Pohalton Lake

Thick heavy leaves of emerald lie
    Upon Pohalton's water's blue,
    O'erspread with lustrous drops of dew,
Dashed from my oar, as I glide by
    In my swift light canoe.   5

Large water-lilies, virtue-pure,
    Bright stars that with Pohalton fell
    From heaven where the angels dwell,
Drive back the shadows that obscure,
    And, siren-like, my fancies lure.   10

Unmindful of the moccasin
    That, swift with darting tongue, slips by
    And climbs a sunny drift to dry,
Reposing half awake, his tawny skin
    Scarce revealed to the searching eye.   15

Huge frightened turtles disappear;
    And as the ripples widen o'er
    The lake toward the reedy shore,
The dragon-fly, a wise old seer,
    Drops down upon the log to pore—   20

And, ever and anon, the breeze
    From piney mountains far away,
    Steals in; and waters kiss the day,
And break the image of the trees
    That looking downward, sigh dismay.   25

The wood spirit is wandering near,
    Wrapt in old legends' mystery;
    I drift alone, for none but he
And nature's self are native here
    Of me to know. But now I see   30

The patient heron by the shore
    Put down his little leg and fly,
    While echoes from the woods reply
To each uncanny scream, low o'er
    The lake into the evening sky.   35

Vast brooding silence crowds around;
    Dark vistas lead my eye astray
    Among vague shapes beyond the day
Upon the lake, I hear no sound;
    I go ashore, and hasten 'way.   40

Twin Territories 1 (November 1899): 246. According to a note accompanying this version of the poem in *Twin Territories,* it was also published earlier in the *Indian Journal,* but no copy has been found. Along with varying indentation, the version of this poem in the 1910 edition reverses the order of stanzas three and four.

Shelter

In my cabin in the clearing
I lie and hear the Autumn showers pouring slow;
Afar, almost out of hearing,
I lie and hear the wet wind thro' the forest go.

Sense of shelter steals o'er me;   5
Into the evening dimness failing,
Into the night before me,
I lie and fancy I am sailing.

All night the wind will be blowing;
All night the rain will slowly pour,   10
But I shall sleep, never knowing
The storm raps ceaseless at my door.

Muskogee Phoenix, November 2, 1899.

To a Daffodil

When Death has shut the blue skies out from me,
        Sweet Daffodil,
And years roll on without my memory,
Thou'lt reach thy tender fingers down to mine of clay,
        A true friend still, 5
Although I'll never know thee till the Judgment Day.

Muskogee Phoenix, November 2, 1899; also in the *St. Louis Republic*, November 26, 1899.

Happy Times for Me an' Sal

Hear the happy jays a-singin';
    Leaves a-driftin' in the medder;
    See the 'simmons turnin' redder,
An' the farmer boy a-grinnin'
    At his copper toes.   5
    Happy times fer me an' Sal;
    Happy times fer Jim an' Al;
    We've raised a sumshus crop,
    An' we are upon top,
    In our new-bought clothes.   10

More an' more it's gittin' cooler;
    Frost is makin' purtyer picters
    On the winder-panes. By victers!
I am feelin' like a ruler
    Over all this earth.   15
    Happy Happy times fer me an' Sal;
    Happy times fer Jim an' Al;
    We've raised a sumshus crop,
    An' we are upon top,
    Settin' by the he'rth.   20

Nights are havin' longer howers;
    Sleep is surely growin' finer;
    Dreams becomin' sweeter, kiner,
Since the season of the flowers,
    Winter days fer me.   25
    Lots o' time fer Lib'ral thought;
    Lots o' time to worry not;
    When snow's knee-deep out doors;
An' driftin' on the moors,
    Like a silver sea.   30

Undated newspaper clipping, scrapbook, Posey Collection, Gilcrease. What appears to be an earlier version of this poem appears in *Twin Territories* 1 (December 1899): 20. A manuscript of this poem is in folder 140 of the Gilcrease Posey Collection.

[What sea-maid's longings dwell] [To a Sea Shell]

What sea-maid's longings dwell
    Upon thy lips, O Shell,
Washed to my feet from the depths of the sea?
    Listening, I hold thee to my ear,
But the secret that I would hear   5
Blends with the ocean's mystery.

Twin Territories 2 (March 1900): 50. This untitled poem was published as "To a Sea Shell" in the 1910 edition, which most likely takes its title from an earlier manuscript version. See Ledger, folder 140, Posey Collection, Gilcrease.

The Decree

What does the white man say to you?
    Says he, "You've got to hoe; you've got to plow;
    You've got to live by the sweat of your brow—
Even as I. You've held your last powwow
        And your last revelry.   5
The council fire whereby you hold debate
        Against my stern decree
Is flickering out before the breath of fate."

What does the white man say to you?
    Thus speaketh he to you: "You've got to cast   10
    Your laws as relics to an empty past.
You've got to change and mend your ways at last.
        I am your keeper and
Your guardian, in the judgment of mankind,
        And 'tis mine to command   15
You in the way that leaves your savage self behind."

The Red Man 16 (April 1900): 3.

Song of the Oktahutche

Far, far, far are my silver waters drawn;
    The hills embrace me loth to let me go;
The maidens think me fair to look upon,
    And trees lean over glad to hear me flow.
Thro' field and valley, green because of me,   5
    I wander, wander to the distant sea.

Thro' lonely places and thro' crowded ways;
    Thro' noise of strife and thro' the solitude,
And on thro' cloudy days and sunny days,
    I journey till I meet, in sisterhood,   10
The broad Canadian, red with the sunset,
    Now calm, now raging in a mighty fret!

On either hand, in a grand colonnade,
    The cottonwoods rise in the azure sky,
And purple mountains cast a purple shade   15
    As I, now grave, now laughing, pass them by;
And birds of air dip bright wings in my tide,
    In sunny reaches where I noiseless glide.

O'er shoals of mossy rocks and mussel shells,
    Blue over spacious beds of amber sand,   20
By cliffs and coves and glens where Echo dwells—
    Elusive spirit of the shadow-land—
Forever blest and blessing, do I go,
    A wid'ning in the morning's roseate glow.

Though I sing my song in a minor key, 25
　　Broad lands and fair attest the good I do;
Though I carry no white sails to the sea,
　　Towns nestle in the vales I wander thro';
And quails are whistling in the waving grain,
　　And herds are scattered o'er the verdant plain. 30

Sturm's Oklahoma Magazine 1 (1906): 92. An identical version of this poem on an undated newspaper clipping in a scrapbook is held in the Gilcrease Posey Collection. An earlier version appeared in *Twin Territories* 2 (May 1900): 87. An undated manuscript of this poem can be found on two sheets of Eufaula High School stationery in folder 154 of the Gilcrease Posey Collection, and this version was probably written between the fall of 1899 and the early months of 1900. The version found in the 1910 edition spells "Oktahutche" as "Oktahutchee." While spellings of Muscogee words certainly vary, Posey always wrote the word with a single "e." As the version presented in this edition was the last published during Posey's lifetime, it probably best reflects his wishes. Oktahutche is the Muscogee name for the North Canadian River in eastern Oklahoma. Translated, the name means "Sand Creek."

Line 11: The Canadian River.
Line 21: In Greek mythology, Echo is a nymph who is deprived by Hera of her ability to speak and must instead repeat the words of others.

To a Robin

Out in the Golden air,
Out where the skies are fair,
I hear a song of gladness,
With never a note of sadness.
Ring out thy heart's delight, 5
And mine of every sorrow!
Sing, sweet bird, till the night,
And come again tomorrow.

Sturm's Oklahoma Magazine 1 (October 1905): 84. An identical version of this poem, on an undated newspaper clipping, is in a scrapbook held at the Gilcrease Posey Collection. Slightly different versions of this poem appeared in *Twin Territories* 4 (September 1902): 258; and *Twin Territories* 2 (July 1900): 139. The version of this poem in the 1910 edition has different indentations and other minor variations. As the version presented here is the last one known from Posey's lifetime, it probably best reflects his wishes.

Bob White

A speck of brown adown the dusty pathway runneth he.
Then whirreth, like a missle shot, into a neighboring tree.
  Bob-Bob White!

The joyous call comes like a silver chime.
And back across the fields of summer time,   5
  The echo, faint but sweetly clear,
Falls dying on the list'ning ear—
  Bob-Bob White!

And when the cheery voice is dead,
  And silence soothes the wind to rest,   10
Among the oak boughs overhead,
  From valley, hill or meadow's breast,
There comes an answering call—
  Bob-Bob White!
And, once more, over all,   15

The spirit Silence weaves her spell,
  And light and shadow play
At hide-and-seek behind the high
  Blue walls around the day.
Again, from where the wood and prairie meet,   20
Across the tasseled corn and waving wheat,
Awak'ning many tender memories sweet—
  Bob-Bob White!

Sturm's Oklahoma Magazine 1 (October 1905): 85. An identical version of this poem can be found in an undated newspaper clipping in a scrapbook held in the Gilcrease Posey Collection. This poem was also published in slightly different versions in *Twin Territories* 4 (October 1902): frontispiece; and *Twin Territories* 2 (August 1900): 172. The version of this poem in the 1910 edition reprints the lines in a significantly different order from any known version from his lifetime. As the version presented here is the last known to have been published during Posey's lifetime, it probably best reflects his wishes. What is probably the first manuscript of this poem can be found on Eufaula High School stationery in folder 147 of the Gilcrease Posey Collection.

The Blue Jay

The silence of the golden afternoon
    Is broken by the chatter of the jay.
    What season finds him when he is not gay,
Light-hearted, noisy, singing out of tune,
High-crested, blue as is the sky of June?   5
    'Tis autumn when he comes; the hazy air.
    Half-hiding like a veil, lies ev'rywhere,
Full of memories of summer soon
To fade; leaves, losing hold upon the tree,
    Fly helpless in the wintry wind's unrest;   10
The goldenrod is burning low and fitfully;
    The squirrel leaves his leafy summer nest,
Descends and gathers up the nuts that drop,
When lightly shaken, from the hick'ry top.

The Red Man and Helper, September 7, 1900. This poem is also in an undated manuscript on Eufaula High School stationery, folder 145, Posey Collection, Gilcrease.

Moonlight [In the Moonlit Wood]

I dream that it is snowing
    And waking do but find
The moonbeams softly glowing
    Thro' branches intertwined.

St. Louis Republic, November 26, 1900; see an undated clipping, scrapbook, Posey Collection, Gilcrease. This poem is titled "In the Moonlit Wood" in the 1910 edition.

The Haunted Valley

Ever, somewhere in the boundless blue,
    Floats a cloud, like a ship at sea;
Ever a shadow lies on the hills
    And a wind from the South blows free

Ever is heard the voice of the pines   5
    As they weep o'er a long-lost love
And ever, like the path of a star,
    Flows the stream with hills above

Ever the glens betray, passing sweet,
    Secrets of brown lovers no more   10
Ever the huntsman lingering there
    At eve hears the dip of the oar

Beholds on the moonlit wave afar,
    Two vague forms in a light canoe
That is lost anon in the shadow   15
    Where the river bends out of view.

Undated manuscript on Wetumka National School stationery, folder 155, Posey Collection, Gilcrease. Posey held the position of superintendent of the Wetumka National School between June 1900 and the spring of 1901 (Littlefield, *Alex Posey*, 116–22). By the time he took this job, his poetic output had waned significantly. While he continued to publish his earlier poems, "The Haunted Valley" is Posey's only known poem to have been written during this period.

On the Capture and Imprisonment of Crazy Snake

Down with him! chain him! bind him fast!
    Slam to the iron door and turn the key!
The one true Creek, perhaps the last
    To dare declare, "You have wronged me!"
Defiant, stoical, silent,   5
    Suffers imprisonment!

Such coarse black hair! such eagle eye!
    Such stately mien!—how arrow-straight!
Such will! such courage to defy
    The powerful makers of his fate!   10
A traitor, outlaw,—what you will,
    He is the noble red man still.

Condemn him and his kind to shame!
    I bow to him, exalt his name!

The Poems of Alexander Lawrence Posey, comp. Minnie H. Posey (Topeka: Crane, 1910), 88. There is no copy of this poem dating from Alexander Posey's lifetime; as Minnie H. Posey sometimes altered her husband's work, this version may not reflect his wishes. In the 1910 edition, the title of this poem reads "On the Capture and Imprisonment of Crazy Snake, January 1900," but this title is incorrect because Chitto Harjo was not imprisoned until January 1901. For this edition the title has been truncated to correct this error, which probably stems from a mistake by Minnie Posey. Chitto Harjo (Crazy Snake) (1846–1911?) was the charismatic Muscogee (Creek) traditionalist leader who in 1901 led the so-called Snake Uprising when he and his followers formed their own government at the Muscogee town of Hickory Ground. They resisted the loss of tribal sovereignty and traditional ways that accompanied the workings of the Dawes Commission. In January 1901 their mostly peaceful "uprising" was quickly put down and Chitto along many of his followers (called "Snakes" by their detractors) were briefly imprisoned. Chitto Harjo and his fellow conservatives remained strongly opposed to the allotment of land, with many never accepting their own allotments (Chaudhuri and Chaudhuri 64; Debo 376; Womack 146).

The Fall of the Redskin

(With apologies to Edwin Markham)

Awed by the laws of Arkansaw, the whims
Of Hitchcock, and the bill that Curtis sent
To him, he leans against a witness tree
And gazes on the far-blazed section-line,
The emptiness of treaties in his face, 5
And on his back the burden of the squaw.
Who made him dead to raptures of the chase,
The ills of not desiring to allot,
A thing opposed to change, that never files,
Stubborn and slow, a brother to the Boer? 10
Who loosened and let down the pledge—
"As long as streams give tribute to the sea,
And grass spreads yearly banquet for the herds?
Whose breath blew out the faith within this brain?
Is this the thing the Lord God made and gave 15
To have dominion over sea and land;
To hunt the deer and chase the buffalo
From climes of snow to climes beneath the sun?"
Is this the dream He dreamed who shaped Tom Platt
And sent Roosevelt on his career of light? 20
Down all the stretch of Carpetbaggers to
The last man fresh from Maine or Illinois,
There shines no ray of hope for him! He sees
But darkness filled with censure of his ways—
Night filled with signs and portents that appall— 25
Greed fraught with menace to his grass and ore!

What gulf between him and home rule! The ward
Of Uncle Sam's high-salaried minions,
What to him are Tams Bixby, J. George Wright?
What the long reaches of the tape of red,   30
The splendors of the carpetbag regime?
Through this dread shape the Filipino looks;
The vow not kept is in that doubting stare;
Through this dread shape humanity betrayed,
Plundered, profaned and disinherited,   35
Cries protest to the judges of the courts,
A protest that is also made in vain.

O, Bill McKinley, Hanna, bosses in
All lands Republican beyond dispute,
How will you reckon with this Indian in   40
That hour when he unchallenged casts his vote,
When whirlwinds of Democracy blow J.
Blair Shoenfelt back north to see the folks,
And spiders weave their nets in spacious rooms
And corridors of Misrule's capital?   45

How will it be with towns that batten on
The wrong—with those whose bread depends upon
The shame—when Bradford's dream becomes a fact
And pies of politics are baked at home?

Indian Journal, January 18, 1901. This poem was also published in the January 24, 1901, issue of the *Wagoner Record* under the title "The Man with the Woe." This poem parodies the Edwin Markham (1852–1840) poem, "The Man with the Hoe," which was published in 1899 and enjoyed wide popularity. Posey would again parody this same Markham poem in his 1906 poem "The Creek Fullblood."

Line 1: As Oklahoma statehood approached, the United States imposed the state laws of the neighboring state of Arkansas upon the various American Indian nations of Indian Territory. This move furthered the transition from tribal to state government and, as this poem suggests, was not a popular change even among those who considered themselves "progressives."

Line 2: Ethan Allen Hitchcock (1835–1909), U.S. Secretary of the Interior. Charles Curtis (1860–1936), congressman and author of the Curtis Act. He would later become vice president under Herbert Hoover.

Line 10: Boer, a reference to the Dutch, who after establishing the South African republic fought the English, who wanted to control the gold-wealthy area. The Boer War officially lasted from 1899 to 1902.

Line 19: Thomas Collier Platt (1833–1910), the senator responsible for an amendment to an army appropriations bill that persuaded Cubans to draft a constitution providing the United States the right to become involved in the decisions of the Cuban government.

Line 20: Theodore Roosevelt (1858–1919), at this time vice president of the United States. Roosevelt's involvement in the Spanish-American War, particularly with his so-called Rough Riders, had significantly boosted his popularity.

Line 29: Tams Bixby (1855–1922), congressman from Minnesota who was the chairman of the Dawes Commission. J. George Wright (1860–1941) was the Indian inspector for Indian Territory at the time of this poem's composition.

Line 38: William McKinley (1843–1901) was serving his second term as president of the United States at the time of this poem's publication. He would be assassinated a few months later, on September 14, 1901. Marcus Alonzo Hanna (1837–1904) was an Ohio senator who spearheaded both of McKinley's presidential campaigns.

Line 43: J. Blair Shoenfelt (1859–1905) was the United States agent to the Five Civilized Tribes at the time of this poem.

Line 48: According to Daniel F. Littlefield Jr., this is probably Gamaliel Bradford (1831–1911), a Massachusetts banker who detailed his anti-republication political ideas in a book titled *The Lesson of Popular Government* (1899).

Fus Harjo and Old Billy Hell

    Fus Harjo was not a good Creek;
        The pious members of his clan
    Declared his virtues all were weak;
        That Satan daily led the man;
For when they pitched their tents to feast and praise the Lord
with zest,   5
He pitched his at the Square and in the dance led all the rest.

    So when the news was spread one day
        That Fus had bought a violin,
    The church folks straightaway ceased to pray
        For him, shocked at so great a sin.   10
He gave the Indian trader for the instrument
A quit-claim to his head-right money, every cent.

    When he had touched the trader's pen
        And made the usual Christian sign,
    He took his brand new fiddle then   15
        And got himself on a bee-line
Immediately, for fear the trader, if he stayed,
Perchance, might want to rue the trade that he had made.

    Fus Harjo set himself to saw;
        He sawed thro' weather foul and fair;   20
    If he'd been sawing wood, his squaw
        Would not have known a daily care;
No doubt, he would have sawed until his head was gray
Had it not dawned upon him that he could not play.

"Perhaps, the prophet Chalogee, 25
    Who does most anything you want,
  Can learn me how to play," said he,
    And straightway sought the wise man's haunt,
"I would, Harjo, that you had come to me for rain,"
The prophet answered him, "I fear you've come in vain. 30

"For, tho' I know the rainbow well—
    Can bid it come or bid it go—
  It happens, I regret to tell,
    I know naught of your fiddle bow.
However, I can set you on a certain clue 35
That may to very wonderful results lead you."

"I have some due-bills for your clue,"
    Said Harjo, very much relieved.
  "Will one for half a dollar do?"
    This prodigal reward received 40
The prophet Chalogee began, most grave and slow:
"Remember, then, upon a journey must you go

"By night until the morning star
    Shines on you in the loneliest part
  Of Tulledega mountains far. 45
    You needs must go forth stout of heart,
For you shall hear unearthly noises everywhere,
And in the unstarred darkness meet the Devil there.

"To him thus shall you make address:
    'Thou god of darkness and of sin, 50
  Fus Harjo, famed for wickedness,
    Would learn to play the violin.'"
When Harjo said, "I little like your clue, O seer,"
The prophet Chalogee gave answer, "Have no fear.

"You'll find my clue to be first rate; 55
 'Twill make you famous in the land;
Besides—but it is growing late,
 And I've a shower on my hand."
The conference coming thus abruptly to an end,
Fus Harjo sought the pathway home, down in Bear Bend. 60

Fus Harjo bade his squaw to pound
 Him some apusky—'bout a quart—
To cook some dumplings—blue and sound—
 A slice of beef—the sun-dried sort—
A rarer dish that which, when hashed, I mind not one! 65
"Have these," said Harjo, "ready by the set of sun."

Not satisfied till each parched grain
 Of maize turns into golden dust,
The good squaw pounds with might and main
 Exactly as all good squaws must. 70
She boils the dumpling, cooks the beef, while Harjo lies
Beneath the arbor like catalpa, fighting flies.

As Tulledega lay a bank
 Of purple 'gainst the fading sky
Fus Harjo, rising ate and drank; 75
 And then, without explaining why,
Took up his brand new instrument but frazzled bow
And vanished like a spectre in the afterglow.

He traveled on and on along
 By ways uncertain thro' the night, 80
Now in the open, now among
 The trees, now up, or down, the height
He stumbled here or yonder fell into a mire
And, though his fiddle saved, his temper lost entire.

>He took a short cut here and there
>>A shorter still, to save his strength;
>For he would have no strength to spare
>>If, when he reached the goal at length,
>Old Nick should try to play him foul. Sometimes a limb
>Scraped on his fiddle and almost frightened him.

>At last, he came to Limbo, brook
>>Of dismal name, coiled at the base
>Of Tulledega. There he took
>>Refreshments, then resumed his pace.
>Up, up the mountain, thro' the dark pinewoods went he;
>Then down, far down into the vale of mystery.

>He rested near the boulder grey
>>Of strange inscriptions—near the place
>A lonely huntsman fell a prey
>>To wolves, o'ertaken in the race.
>He heard the river chafing on the rocks below,
>The pines complain as night winds rocked them to an fro.

>Then all at once an earthquake's shock
>>The whole world jarred, and stars went out,
>And tree crushed tree, and rock crushed rock,
>>And frenzied winds came with a shout,
>And shallow waters in the river leaped to drown!
>Behold, Fus Harjo's hair stood up instead of down!

>Then something did so roughly poke
>>Him in the ribs he jumped sidewise,
>Thought he heard one rib when it broke,
>>The punch one meant to paralyze.
>The pain shot up and down his spine and he was dumb,
>But knew that Billy Hell had jabbed him with his thumb.

"Thou god of darkness and of sin, 115
    Fus Harjo, famed for wickedness,
Would learn to play the violin,"
    Said Harjo, trembling more or less.
Whereupon Nick took his instrument without reply,
Examined it closely and ran the strings up high, 120

A-thrumming each now loud now low,
    To get the pure and perfect sound.
Then, with a flourish of the bow,
    And stamping his hoof on the ground,
Nick gave Fus such a shower-bath of melodies 125
As lifted him to highest glory by degrees.

What runs! what tremulous thrill! and O
    What variation did he play!
At each unseen touch of the bow,
    Yet finer runs and trills held sway, 130
And variations, vastly better than the last,
Held Harjo and the warring elements steadfast!

"Now let me hear you play," said Nick
    Returning Fus his instrument.
"It is a very simple trick," 135
    But Fus the air with discords rent,
Whereat Nick lost his temper, scratched Fus on the head,
Stampeded over him, and left him all but dead!

When Fus Harjo, at last, came to,
    With aches and pains in every limb, 140
Chilled thro' and wringing wet with dew,
    Nick's hoof-prints were all over him!
Some forty yards apart his bow and fiddle lay
And his apusky was scattered every-which-way!

    He picked up his apusky sack, 145
        Put in his violin and bow,
    Slinging the burden o'er his back
        He went home straighter than a crow,
As bright day came extinguishing night's lesser lights
And south-born breezes freshened o'er the piney heights. 150

    But for the prophet Chalogee,
        The magic healer of all ails,
    Who gave him much yalonka tea—
        A remedy that never fails,
Even tho' Nick be responsible for its use— 155
Fus Harjo would not have lived over his abuse.

    Then spake the prophet Chalogee,
        "I charge you now to not complain;
    Good lies deeper than we can see;
        Trees flourish from a hidden grain. 160
As I've given you bitter draughts to make you well,
So Nick his blows that you in music might excel."

    "I lived long weeks and did not eat;
        Alone kept fierce beasts company;
    Passed perils few would dare to meet, 165
        To win the gift of prophecy,
The power to uproot all causes of disease,
Make drouthy summers green, and probe the mysteries."

    At this each lingering ache and sore
        In Fus let go; the old desire 170
    Returned grown stronger than of yore;
        He smote the strings with soul on fire,
With feet a-patting, playing tunes not heard before,
Henceforth, Fus played at every dance the country o'er.

Indian Journal, March 22, 1901.

Line 1: Fus Harjo, translated from Muscogee, means "Crazy Bird." This name appears to be an evolutionary link between Alexander Posey's "Chinnubbie Harjo" pen name and his "Fus Fixico" persona. He never used the name of "Fus Harjo" again in his writing.

Line 6: The tribal town square was the location of the "stomp" dances and other activities associated with the Muscogee Green Corn Ceremony.

Line 12: A quit-claim relinquished a person's holding of certain property. In this context Posey probably refers to the character's share of Muscogee national assets (note courtesy Daniel F. Littlefield Jr.).

Line 40: Another term for a check or I. O. U.

Line 41: Chalogee, a medicine man Posey knew as a child. For another of Posey's tales about this real life figure see "Two Famous Prophets" in Posey, *Chinnubbie and the Owl*, 67–72.

Line 62: Apusky is a traditional Muscogee food made from corn meal.

Line 63: Blue dumplings are another traditional Muscogee food made from corn.

Line 91: A creek found near Posey's early childhood home of the Tulledega region west of present-day Eufaula, Oklahoma.

Line 98: According to Daniel F. Littlefield Jr., this passage refers to actual petroglyphs found in the Tulledega Hills area.

Line 153: A medicinal tea.

Saturday

To my friend Jim Cowin

Danged, if I kin be content 'roun'
    Home on Saterday—gits me down.
It's a day to smoke cigyars on,
    Hear tall talk an' see airs on,
A day to gas an' whittle on,   5
    Maybe, take a little on!

Jes 'pears like Sunday when you stay
    'Bout home, glum like, on Saterday.
Somehow it gits me out o' hitch,
    Gives me the all-overs an' sich   10
Till I saddle old Jude an' set
    Her clean to town in a fret.

I jes can't he'p but go to town
    On Saterday, an' loaf aroun'
It's a day to git the news on,   15
    To play at cards an' lose on;
It's a day for folks to meet on,
    To spark the gal you're sweet on.

It's jes in me to be in town
    On Saterday, a mozin' 'round'   20
It's a day to trade an' swap on,
    To soak your hoss an' crop on.
It's a day to have your fun on,
    To get your grindin' done on.

Don't keer if it pours down for weeks,   25
    On Saterday I'll head the creeks!
It's a day to go to town on,
    The folks you know ar' foun' on:
It's a day to git home late on,
    Have the ol' woman wait on.   30

I never missed but once to go,
    An' jacks I felt worse a week er mo'.
It's a day one ort not pick on
    To complain an' be sick on.
It's a day to get up soon on,   35
    An' ride to town 'fore noon on.

Ginst one Saterday passes by,
    Anuther's loomin' in my eye.
It's a day to Jew an' buy on—
    I mean the things they're high on—   40
To take the editor's hint on,
    Pay up an' git in print on.

My plow, when Saterday comes 'roun',
    Kin stand till Monday in the groun'
It's a day to see the sights on,   45
    To drop in at Abe Kite's on;
A day to eat a tamale on.
    To be in Eufaly on!

Indian Journal, March 22, 1901. The Cowins lived near Posey's Bald Hill residence and rented land from him in 1897; see Posey, "Journal of the Creek Orphan Asylum," February 3, 4, and 5, 1897.

Line 46: Abe Kite was a Eufaula hide dealer. See Posey, "Journal of the Creek Orphan Asylum," February 3, 1897.

Line 47: Tamale vendors were commonly found in Indian Territory towns (note courtesy of Daniel F. Littlefield Jr.)

The Evening Star

Behold, Evening's bright star,
Like a door left ajar
In God's mansion afar,
    Over the mountain's crest
    Throws a beautiful ray— 5
A sweet kiss to the day,
As he sinks to his rest.

Sturm's Oklahoma Magazine 1 (October 1905): 84. A version of this poem, with minor differences in indentation, was published in *Twin Territories* 4 (March 1902): 65.

On Hearing a Redbird Sing

Out in the howling wind;
Out in the falling snow;
Out in the blight and gloom
Of a desolate world,
I hear a lone bird sing,   5
"O it is sweet, sweet, sweet!"

Out in the sunless fields;
Out in the moaning woods;
Out in the dark and cold
Of a drear stricken world,   10
   I see the roses bloom
     And hear the drop of leaves!

Twin Territories 4 (March 1902): 84.

She Was Obdurate

A young Southern gentleman, who visited his mother in this city a short time since, writes back thus:

"I had a very uneventful trip all the way back. A very pretty girl got on the train at South McAlester and occupied the seat just in front of me. I of course had to help her raise the window, but she didn't invite me over to sit with her, as I thought she should have done, although I fumbled around with it considerably longer than necessary. She wore a hat trimmed with a wreath of violets, and pretty soon the wind blew off a small spray which fell in my lap, and I leaned over and asked her if I might have them, which she agreed to, but immediately relapsed into an oysterlike silence, so I wrote a verse and dropped it over into her lap, which in order to preserve for the delectation of posterity, I will here repeat:

'Where are you going, my pretty maid?
I would have asked, but I was afraid,
When I helped you raise the window shade.
I have seldom seen a face so fair,
And 'tis many a trip since such hair
Has trailed o'er the back of a 'Katy' chair.
I miss the violet's sweet perfume,
But thank the wind that stole the bloom.'

"I signed it 'Chinnubbie Harjo' and went into the next car in order to see if she would greet me with a 'spasm' when I returned, but we had passed Denison when I came back, and she must have gotten off there, for she was absent. I immediately proceeded to calm my wildly palpitating heart, swallowed my vain tears, and dashed away the lump in my throat which was struggling for exit, and busied myself with the biscuits and 'preserves' with which your forethought had provided me, ruminating the while, on the transitory nature of human events."

It's our set 'em up.

Indian Journal, May 23, 1902. The setting is the passenger train the "Katy Flyer."

What a Snap

I wish I were an editor,
Out in the country free,
Where old subscribers would bring
Potatoes in to me;
And as I counted up each spud, 5
Each cabbage and each beet,
I grab my pen and give the man
    A veg'table receipt.

Indian Journal, June 26, 1903.

It's Too Hot

He hates to sweat
Does Bill Mellette.
   He'll wait till frost, no doubt;
It's too hot yet
For Bill Mellette   5
To turn the rascals out.

Indian Journal, August 14, 1903. This poem also appeared in *Fort Smith Times*, August 19, 1903.

Line 1: In 1903 accusations surfaced that federal officials and some members of the Dawes Commission were involved in illegal land dealings. Concerned citizens demanded that William Mellette, the U.S. attorney in charge of the area, call a grand jury investigation of the matter. Mellette initially declined because he said it was too hot to convene a jury. Eventually the investigation did occur, finding several federal employees guilty of land fraud. See Littlefield, *Alex Posey*, 175–76.

Alex Posey is Responsible

A recent snap shot of President Roosevelt shows him tipping his hat to a friend standing near a billboard on which was a large poster advertising the gold dust twins (negro babies). This causes the Muskogee Times poet to break forth with:

If Hitchcock goes off half cocked,
    And Bony closes up like a clam,
While Roosevelt tips his hat to the Gold Dust Twins,
    How old is Mary Ann?

Undated clipping, scrapbook, Posey Collection, Gilcrease. Due to its subject matter, Posey probably wrote the poem referred to in this brief newspaper piece in the fall of 1903 while he was the editor of the *Muskogee Times*.

Line 3: The N. K. Fairbanks Company advertised several of their cleansing products with racist caricatures of two African American children. These children were called the Gold Dust Twins and were often displayed doing various household chores below the catch-phrase of "let the twins do your work."

Line 5: Ethan Allen Hitchcock (1835–1909), secretary of the Interior. In 1903 allegations arose that a number of federal employees and members of the Dawes Commission were involved in land graft. In October of 1903, Hitchcock appointed Charles Joseph Bonaparte (1851–1921), a lawyer from Maryland, to investigate the allegations. Posey was critical of Bonaparte, who conducted his cursory investigation behind closed doors (hence "closes up like a clam") and did little to punish those involved in the illegal land dealings. See Littlefield, *Alex Posey*, 180–83, and Posey, *The Fus Fixico Letters*, 138n.

Line 6: Boney, Posey's humorous nickname for Charles Joseph Bonaparte.

Line 8: Mary Ann is unidentified.

A Freedman Rhyme

Now de time fer ter file
Fer yo' Freedman chile.
You bettah lef' dat watermelon 'lone
An' go look up some vacant lan'
Fer all dem chillun what you t'ink is yone.　　　　5
De good lan' aint a-gwine ter last
Twell Gabul blow de Judgment blast.
Hits miltin' like snow
Up eroun' Bristow;
Dey'll be none lef' but rocks an' river san'.　　　　10
De Injun filin' mighty fast;
Bettah hump Yo'se'r, nigger,
An' gin ter kin' 'o figger.

—FUS FIXICO

Muskogee Democrat, August 19, 1905. In this poem Posey derides those Muscogee freed people who, during the allotment process, signed up for their share of land. This poem makes plain Posey's racist tendencies and also betrays his disdain for allotment rules that allowed Muscogee freed people the same right to land as other members of the Muscogee Nation.

The Creek Fullblood

(With apologies to Edwin Markham)

Shorn of his rights for centuries he mopes
Beside his hut and broods upon his plight,
The emptiness of treaties in his face,
And in his morose soul an outraged trust.
Who made him pretty to grafter and the shark,   5
A thing that any rogue may rob that will,
Hold up and plunder in the open day?
Who conceived the undoing of this Creek?
Whose was the act that forced this change on him?
Who trampled under foot his sacred rights?   10
Is this the Creek to whom was granted sole
Dominion over all this western land?
What gulfs between him and that solemn pledge!
Prey of the horde of grafters, what to him
Are Hitchcock and the swing of the Big Stick?   15
What the long reaches of the tape of red,
The rules prescribed, restrictions on his land?
Through this red man the Filipino looks;
The faith not kept is in that doubting stare;
Through this Poor Lo humanity betrayed,   20
Plundered, profaned and disinherited,
Cries protest that is also made in vain.
How will the new state reckon with this Creek?
How answer his blunt questions in that hour
When fate of parties fall into his hand?   25
How will it be with bosses, cliques and rings—
With those who shaped him to the thing he is—
When this Indian shall answer at the polls,
After the silence of the centuries?

Muskogee Times-Democrat, August 9, 1906. Like "The Fall of the Redskin," this poem parodies Edwin Markham's then-famous poem, "The Man with the Hoe."

Line 15: Ethan Allen Hitchcock (1835–1909), secretary of the Interior. Big Stick is a reference to Theodore Roosevelt's approach to foreign affairs, made famous by his adage that the United States should "speak softly and carry a big stick."

Line 18: Here Posey conflates the situation of the American Indians with that of the Filipinos, whom he suggests the United States betrayed by denying them self-rule after the Spanish-American War. This opinion may derive from the United States putting down Emilio Aguinaldo's 1902 insurrection. (This note courtesy of Daniel F. Littlefield Jr.)

Line 20: Many Indian Territory journalists sarcastically called conservative American Indians "Poor Lo." This name derived from a poem by Alexander Pope, called "Essay on Man," that reads in part: "Lo, the poor Indian! whose untutor'd mind / Sees God in clouds, or hears him in the wind." (This note courtesy of Daniel F. Littlefield Jr.)

Arkansaw

(The insinuation that nothing would rhyme with Arkansas has stirred the ire of the local poets and one of them comes forward with a defense.)

No rhyme for Arkansaw?
What's wrong with mother-in-law,
Or Wichita,
Or Washita,
Or Spavinaw, 5
Or Mackinaw,
Or Ma
And Pa?

Bah!
Hath not a crow a caw,
And greedy sharks a maw? 10
Is not a female Chickasaw
A squaw?
Don't jacks hee-haw
And wildcats claw?
Ever hear of Esau? 15
Never saw
A Choctaw
Smoke or chaw?
Ever see a Quapaw 20
Eating a ripe pawpaw?

No rhyme for Arkansaw?
Pshaw!

Muskogee-Times Democrat, June 20, 1907. This poem also appeared in the June 29, 1907, issue of the *Tahlequah Arrow*, and in the July 5, 1907, issue of the *Indian Journal*.

Checotah

There was a small town, Checotah
A very nice place to gotah,
    'Till the farmers got skinned
     On the cotton there ginned
And rose in their might and smotah.   5

Indian Journal, May 1, 1908. Like "O'Blenness," this poem promotes Eufaula as the town best equipped to serve as county seat.

O'Blenness

There was an editor, O'Blenness,
Subsequent cognomen, Dennis.
    Who gave as his quota
    One vote to Checotah,
And his folks approached him with menace.   5

Indian Journal, May 8, 1908. Dennis O'Blenness was the editor of the *Hoffman Herald*, and had promoted the town of Checotah, instead of Posey's town of Eufaula, for county seat. Like "Checotah," this poem is meant to advocate Eufaula as the best town for county seat.

Hotgun on the Death of Yadeka Harjo

"Well, so," Hotgun he say,
    "My ol'-time frien', Yadeka Harjo, he
Was died the other day,
    An' they was no ol'-timer left but me.

"Hotulk Emathla he   5
    Was go to be good Injin long time 'go,
An' Woxie Harjoche
    Been dead ten years or twenty, maybe so.

"All had to die at las';
    I live long time, but now my days was few;   10
'Fore long poke weeds an' grass
    Be growin' all aroun' my grave house, too."

Wolf Warrior listens close,
    An' Kono Harjo pay close 'tention too;
Tookpafka Micco he almos'   15
    Let his pipe go out a time or two.

Kansas City Star, January 19, 1908; also in *Sturm's Oklahoma Magazine* 6 (May 1908): 43. Based on a real man, Hotgun is a character from Posey's "Fus Fixico" letters. Yadeka Harjo was a conservative Muscogee from Hickory Ground, whom Posey visited in October 1905. See Littlefield, *Alex Posey*, 201–2.

Line 5: Hotulk Emathla, second chief of the Muscogee Nation in 1895. He appointed Posey as the superintendent of the Creek Orphan Asylum; see Littlefield, *Alex Posey*, 74, 76, 78, 79.

Line 7: Woxie Harjoche is unidentified.

Line 12: Traditional Muscogee burial customs call for a small house-like structure to be placed over the grave.

Lines 13–15: Wolf Warrior, Kono Harjo, and Tookpafka Micco are fictional characters found in Posey's "Fus Fixico" letters.

Again

Do all the beauteous sunsets glow
And all the fragrant flowers blow
    But on the border line of Bliss?

Is there diviner joy somewhere
That worldly mortals cannot share 5
    Beyond the rapture of a kiss?

If not, why do we dream, when we
Behold the sunsets wane, or see
    The rose in bloom, that there is?

If not, the lovers long in vain 10
That they will meet and kiss again
    In endless lanes of Paradise.

Undated clipping, scrapbook, Posey Collection, Gilcrease.

All the While [Let Men Dispute]

Let mankind fight and jower
    Over creeds decayed or new;
Deny that God had power,
    That the Holy Book is true,
The birds are singing all the while,   5
And grass is growing mile on mile.

Undated clipping, scrapbook, Posey Collection, Gilcrease. An undated manuscript of this poem is in folder 158 of the same collection. The manuscript page also contains the poem "A Vision of June." In Minnie Posey's 1910 edition this poem is titled "Let Men Dispute," but as Minnie sometimes changed her husband's poems, the title from that suspect edition is placed in brackets after the title found in the clipping.

[By the cardinal led aright]

By the cardinal led aright,
    Down the slope of the wild mountainside
    Come the grasses a thirst to my tide;
    As I fall on the rocks at night,
    Far away, like the roar in the shell of the sea,   5
    The weird voice of the pines in the crag answers me
    Here the sky
    Comes to lie
    On my breast
    There the night   10
    In her flight
    From the light
    On the height
    Seeks to rest
'Tis a long away   15
From the hills of the old Dowdie Ranch
    And the valley of pine where I branch
And I murmur all day
    Impatient of delay

Undated manuscript, folder 161, Posey Collection, Gilcrease. Note the similarity of this poem with "[Every moment I flow]," "Esapahutche [Limbo]," and "On Piney." This folder also contains an untitled manuscript version of "Esapahutche [Limbo]."

Line 16: Dowdie Ranch, which Posey also sometimes spelled as "Doughty," "Dawdy," and "Dowdy," is unidentified.

Come

Above,
The stars are bursting into bloom,
My love;
Below, unfolds the evening gloom.
Come, let us roam the long lane thro',   5
My love, just as we used to do.

The birds
Of twilight twitter, sweet and low,
And fly to rest, and honored go
The herds.   10
Come, let the long lane lead us as it will,
My love, a-winding thro' the evening still.

Behold
How now the full-blown stars are spread,
Like large white lilies, overhead!   15
But fold
They must, and fade at gray daylight,
My love; they blossom but at night.

The moon,
My love, uncurls her silv'ry hair,   20
And June
Spills all her sweetness on the air.
Come, let us roam the long lane thro',
My love, just as we used to do.

The Poems of Alexander Lawrence Posey, comp. Minnie H. Posey (Topeka: Crane, 1910), 98–99. There is no copy of this poem dating from Alexander Posey's lifetime; as Minnie H. Posey sometimes altered her husband's work, this version may not reflect his wishes.

The Flower of Tulledega

I know a Tulledegan flower rare
    That lifts between the rocks a blushing face,
And doth with every wind its sweetness share
    That bloweth over its wild dwelling-place.
It gathers beauty where the storms are rough   5
And clings devoted to the rugged bluff.

Far 'bove its sisters in the vale below,
    It swings its censor like a ruby star,
And thither all the days of summer go
    The mountain bees—fierce knights of love and war—   10
To seal in noontide hour—O hour of bliss!—
Each tender vow of true love with a kiss.

And often, like a beauteous blossom blown
    By careless winds o'er heaven's opal floor,
The Butterfly entreats it, "Be my own";   15
    And never would in valleys wander more,
Content to hang for aye enchanted there
Beside the frowning summit bleak and bare.

"Come sit with me in my green cedar tent,
    Bright Flower," said Tulledega long ago,   20
Whilst leaning o'er his lofty battlement,
    And wooed the flower from the vale below.
In vain the Oktahutchee pleaded, "Stay:
    Abide here by my mossy brink always,"

And flashed on thro' the folded hills. "Abide,"   25
    The Valley said, "Upon my verdant breast."
"'Tis bleak and cold up there," the Thrushes cried.
    "Nay, nay, I love the Tulledega best,"
Replied the lovely Flower as it went
High up the Mountain's rugged battlement.   30

"Alas!" the River sighed, and cast a tear
    Upon a slender reed; while overhead
A passing cloud cast down a shadow drear
    Upon the valley green in sunshine spread;
And softly sweet from every feathered throat   35
To music set, escaped a plaintive note.

A chilling breeze came o'er the forest trees,
    And all the leafy branches shook with cold;
Stechupco blew such tender melodies
    As Pan blew from his oaten lute of old,   40
On fair Arcadia's sunny slopes, when Echo
Loved the youth Narcissus to her sorrow.

Abide, O lovely Flower, in your home
    Of pine and cedar on the mountain height;
To come and go, as I have come and gone   45
    So often before,—let that be my delight.
'Tis May, and winds that blow from where you are,
Tell me you hand now like a ruby star.

The Poems of Alexander Lawrence Posey, comp. Minnie H. Posey (Topeka: Crane, 1910), 120–22. There is no copy of this poem dating from Alexander Posey's lifetime; as Minnie H. Posey sometimes altered her husband's work, this version may not reflect his wishes.

Line 1: Tulledega is Posey's name for the rural area west of Eufaula, Muscogee (Creek) Nation, where he spent part of his childhood.

Line 23: Oktahutche is the Muscogee name for the North Canadian River in eastern Oklahoma. Translated, the name means "Sand Creek." As Posey consistently spelled the word "Oktahutche," the spelling presented here is probably a change made by Minnie Posey.

Line 39: Stechupco, also called Este Chupco, is the Muscogee spiritual figure of the "Tall Man," a giant who protects the woodlands. See Chaudhuri and Chaudhuri, *A Sacred Path*, 128–29.

Line 40: In Greek mythology Pan is the god of the forest and fertility who bears the feet, ears, and horns of a goat.

Line 41: Echo is a nymph from Greek myth who falls in love with Narcissus and is then deprived by Hera of her ability to speak and must instead repeat the words of others.

Line 42: In Greek mythology, Narcissus is the handsome son of the river god. Echo falls in love with him, but he rejects her advances.

For Me

I strayed by the shore where the echoes are sleeping
    Among the blue hills that encircle and hide
The broad-breasted river where, laughing and leaping,
    The streamlet makes haste to unite with the tide
Of sylvan Oktaha whose stretches of sand 5
    Made girdles of beauty about this fair land.

The blue of the sky and the green branches waving—
    The sweet invitation of nature to rest
Seem to satisfy all of the soul's eager craving
    To live in a land by eternal spring blest. 10
The mountain, the river, each flower, each tree
    Had a love-song to sing and all, all was for me!

The whispering breeze from the panhandle blowing
    Had breathed on the ripening grain of the west—
Had gathered up sweets where Canadian, flowing 15
    Past cottonwood groves where the summer birds nest,
Low murmured a chorus of rapturous glee
    In vesper-like cadence, and it was for me.

The far-away clouds drifted slowly while seeming
    To blend with the billows of green on the hills 20
Within the cool shade I sat quietly dreaming
    And sipping the nectar the morning distills.
Like mem'ries of love o'er that emerald sea
    The wind-harps of heaven vibrated for me!

Undated clipping, scrapbook, Posey Collection, Gilcrease.

Line 5: A town in what is now Muskogee County in eastern Oklahoma.

Frail Beauty

The raven hair of youth turns gray;
    Bright eyes grow dim; soft cheeks grow pale;
The joyous heart becomes less gay:
    For beauty is a thing so frail,
If once Time's fingers touch it in caress,   5
It droops, and loses all its loveliness.

The Poems of Alexander Lawrence Posey, comp. Minnie H. Posey (Topeka: Crane, 1910), 178. There is no copy of this poem dating from Alexander Posey's lifetime; as Minnie H. Posey sometimes altered her husband's work, this version may not reflect his wishes.

A Glimpse of Spring

Overcast is the sky,
And the wind passes by,
 Breathing blight.
Yet, afar in the gloom,
In the desolate room, 5
 Cold and white,
Where December is king,
I hear a lone bird sing.
 And the gloom,
Ere my glad lips can say, 10
From the earth melts away,
In the warm smile of Spring,
And the frosty winds bring
 Sweet perfume.
In the vast waste of snow, 15
I see the roses bloom.

The Poems of Alexander Lawrence Posey, comp. Minnie H. Posey (Topeka: Crane, 1910), 182. There is no copy of this poem dating from Alexander Posey's lifetime; as Minnie H. Posey sometimes altered her husband's work, this version may not reflect his wishes.

The Homestead of Empire

Lo! plain and sky are brothers; peak
    And cloud confer; the rivers spread
At length to mighty seas!
    The soul is lifted up
In room whose walls share God's; wherein 5
    Empire has staked off a homestead!

Roll on, ye prairies of the west,
    Roll on, like unsailed seas away!
I love thy silence
    And thy mysterious room; 10
Roll on, ye deserts unconfined,
    Roll on into the boundless day!

Roll on, ye rivers of the west,
    Roll on, through canyons to the sea!
Ye chant a harmony 15
    Whereto free people march!
Roll on, O Oregon, roll on!
    Roll on, O thunderous Yosemite!

Ye are the grand voiced singers of
    The great Republic! ye echo 20
Thro' the years the hymn of
    Freedom and of power;
The song of union and of peace
    For aye is in thy troubled flow!

Loom! loom, ye far cold summits of 25
    The west! cloud-girt, snow-crown'd shine on!
Keep watch toward the dawn;
    Keep watch toward the night!
Loom! loom, ye silent sentinels,
    O'er Freedom's vast dominion! 30

Move on, world of the Occident,
    Move on! Thy footfalls thro' the globe
Are heard as thou marchest
    Into that larger day
Whose dawn lights up the armored front 35
    In Cuba and the Philippines.

Undated clipping, scrapbook, Posey Collection, Gilcrease.

[In that valley country lying east]

In that valley country lying east of
'Possum flat, along that clear, cool stream that
Tumbles from the Tulledegan hills, a
Little brook, into the tangled Coon Creek
Woods, and flashes out a river—in that   5
Land of soft blue springs that murmur all the
Year, and where the breezes, scattering fragrance
Stolen from the pine sprays on the westmost
Mountains, whisper what the mocking–bird is
Saying in the sweet June fields, is where I   10
Picked this story up, one quiet sultry
Summer day, when Bald Hill lay aquiv'ring
'Gainst the far horizon in a dreamy haze.

Photocopy of an undated newspaper clipping, box 1-22.6, Littlefield Collection, ANPA. This work appears to introduce a story, but no copy has been found.

Line 2: This is Posey's ranch near Bald Hill; see Littlefield, *Alex Posey*, 96.
Line 3: Tulledega is Posey's name for the rural area west of Eufaula, Muscogee (Creek) Nation, where he spent part of his childhood.
Line 12: Bald Hill, the location of Posey's family ranch near present-day Eufaula, Oklahoma.

Irene

  Irene,
   My queen
Thou dost not love me more.
  Irene,
   My queen,   5
Know my heart is not sore.
  Irene,
   My queen,
Know I can live it o'er.
  Irene,   10
   My queen,
I have been there before.

Undated clipping, scrapbook, Posey Collection, Gilcrease. Irene is unidentified.

On a Marble Medallion of Dante

Close-hooded as a monk;
High-cheeked as a Red Man;
High-nosed as a Hebrew;
Full-lipped as Greek god

The character revealed 5
In this bit of white stone
Is such as is not stamped
Upon a human face
Once in a thousand years

Undated manuscript, folder 157, Posey Collection, Gilcrease.

On the Hills of Dawn

Behold, the morning glory's sky blue cup
Is mine wherewith to drink the nectar up
That morning spills of silver dew
And song upon the winds that woo
And sigh their vows 5
Among the boughs!

Behold, I'm rich in diamonds rare,
And pearls and breathe a golden air
My room is filled with shattered beams
Of light; my life is one of dreams. 10
    In my hut on
      The hills of dawn.

Undated typescript, folder 145, Posey Collection, Gilcrease.

On Viewing the Skull and Bones of a Wolf

How savage, fierce and grim!
    His bones are bleached and white;
But what is death to him?
    He grins as if to bite.
He mocks the fate   5
    That bade, "Begone."
There's fierceness stamped
    In ev'ry bone.
Let silence settle from the midnight sky—
Such silence as you've broken with your cry;   10
The bleak wind howl, unto the utt'most verge
Of this mighty waste, thy fitting dirge.

Undated manuscript, folder 160, Posey Collection, Gilcrease.

Pity

I pity him who never dreams,
    Who has no castles in the air.
Denied my fancies, life would be
    A burden more than I could bear.

I pity him who never hears 5
    The high-born perfect harmony
That haunts the air of loneliness:
    How very dead his soul must be!

I pity him who cannot feel
    The thrill of rapture but in lust; 10
Who cannot rise above himself,
    And only lives because he must.

The Poems of Alexander Lawrence Posey, comp. Minnie H. Posey (Topeka: Crane, 1910), 177. There is no copy of this poem dating from Alexander Posey's lifetime; as Minnie H. Posey sometimes altered her husband's work, this version may not reflect his wishes.

A Reverie

The sky bends over in a sweet
Forgiveness; earth is filled with light;
And mellow autumn hues, soft winds
That croon of summer lands; and thro'
The brooding stillness comes a strain   5
Of music, and, as leaves are swept
Upon the river's tide away,
My thoughts drift off and on to God.

The Poems of Alexander Lawrence Posey, comp. Minnie H. Posey (Topeka: Crane, 1910), 159. There is no copy of this poem dating from Alexander Posey's lifetime; as Minnie H. Posey sometimes altered her husband's work, this version may not reflect his wishes.

The Rural Maid

Said I, "Sweet maid, I do not know your name,
    And you, most sure, a stranger are to me;
But birds sing sweeter for your presence here,—
    My heart is captured by your witchery."

    She fled from me,
    In dread of me.

Said I, "Sweet maid, I did not know your name,
    And you, most sure, a stranger were to me;
But birds sing sadder for your absence here,—
    My heart is broken by your witchery."

The Poems of Alexander Lawrence Posey, comp. Minnie H. Posey (Topeka: Crane, 1910), 116. There is no copy of this poem dating from Alexander Posey's lifetime; as Minnie H. Posey sometimes altered her husband's work, this version may not reflect his wishes.

'Tis Sweet

'Tis sweet, so sweet, when work is o'er,
    At eve, to hear the voice of love
Shout welcome from the cottage door,
    Embowered on the hill above.

From furrowed field, where all day   5
    You toil and sweat for little bread,
'Tis sweet to see the child at play
    Drop toys and come with arms outspread.

The Poems of Alexander Lawrence Posey, comp. Minnie H. Posey (Topeka: Crane, 1910), 152. There is no copy of this poem dating from Alexander Posey's lifetime; as Minnie H. Posey sometimes altered her husband's work, this version may not reflect his wishes.

To My Wife

I've seen the beauty of the rose;
I've heard the music of the bird,
And given voice to my delight;
I've sought the shapes that come in dreams;
I've reached my hands in eager quest,   5
To fold them empty to my breast;
While you, the whole of all I've sought—
The love, the beauty and the dreams—
Have stood, thro' weal and woe, true at
My side silent at my neglect.   10

Undated manuscript, folder 162, Posey Collection, Gilcrease.

To the Indian Meadow Lark

When other birds despairing southward fly,
    In early autumn time away;
When all the green leaves of the forest die,
    How merry still art thou, and gay.

O! golden breasted bird of dawn,   5
    Through all the bleak days singing on,
Till winter, wooed a captive by thy strain,
    Breaks into smiles, and Spring is come again.

Undated clipping, scrapbook, Posey Collection, Gilcrease.

A Valentine

Your cheeks are garden-spots
Of Touch-me-nots;
Your hair the gathered beams
Of sunny dreams;
And that your soul looks thro'   5
Are bits of fallen blue.

No wall hath circled yet,
Nor dews have wet,
A red rose like your lips.
To steal sweet kisses from your brow,   10
A lightsome zephyr I would be,—
A book to murmur you a vow
Of love and constancy.

The Poems of Alexander Lawrence Posey, comp. Minnie H. Posey (Topeka: Crane, 1910), 175. This poem is apparently an amalgamation, possibly made by Minnie Posey herself, of her husband's other poems "Her Beauty" and "To a Face Above the Surf." The first nine lines of "A Valentine" derive from "Her Beauty," and the poem's final four lines are from the first stanza of "To a Face Above the Surf." As there are no copies of "A Valentine" dating from Alexander Posey's lifetime, it is possible that Minnie, in a move similar to one she made in regard to "Distant Music," cobbled this poem together herself for the 1910 edition. See the source note for "Distant Music [early draft]" for more information about Minnie Posey's alterations of the husband's work.

A Vision of Rest

>Some day this quest
>>Shall cease;
>>>Some day,
>>For aye,
>This heart shall rest 5
>>In peace.

Sometimes—ofttimes—I almost feel
The calm upon my senses steal,
So soft, and all but hear
The dead leaves rustle near 10
And sigh to be
At rest with me.
Though I behold
>The ashen branches tossing to and fro,
>>Somehow I only vaguely know 15
The wind is rude and cold.

The Poems of Alexander Lawrence Posey, comp. Minnie H. Posey (Topeka: Crane, 1910), 142. There is no copy of this poem dating from Alexander Posey's lifetime; as Minnie H. Posey sometimes altered her husband's work, this version may not reflect his wishes.

Whence?

Whence come these sweet aeolian airs
Which, in the poet's inmost soul,
Awaken silent melodies?
I asked a wild rose blooming far
Afield, and thus it answered me: 5
"From places like to this, where Love
Abides to start them with his breath."
I questioned then a stately tree,
With leaves a-ripple in the breeze.
"From lonely woods," it gave reply, 10
"Where Sorrow broods uncomforted."
And then I asked a meadow-lark,
A-bobbing on the waving grass,
As quick as blithe, its answer came:
"From meadows where I meet the sun, 15
And brown bees rove in quest of sweets."
Then Tulledega, lying like
A purple shadow in the West,
Gave answer to my question, thus:
"From heights where stormy Passion speaks 20
In the language of the tempest."

Undated manuscript, folder 159, Posey Collection, Gilcrease.

Line 17: Tulledega is Posey's name for the rural area west of Eufaula, Muscogee (Creek) Nation, where he spent part of his childhood.

[With him who lives a neighbor to the birds!]

With him who lives a neighbor to the birds!
Who treasures up the secrets of the woods,
And knows where rivers bend the gracefulest,
Where mountains frown the awfulest and winds
Stray saddest in the forest evergreen!   5
A hut where Limbo drifts the mussel shells ashore.

Undated *Indian Journal* clipping, scrapbook, Posey Collection, Gilcrease.

Line 6: Limbo, a creek found near Posey's early childhood home of the Tulledega region west of present-day Eufaula, Oklahoma.

Appendix

A Ledger of Poems

The manuscript that serves as the source for the ledger poems is a series of pages on 7.5 x 12 in. sheets of ruled paper housed in folder 140 of the Posey Collection of the Gilcrease Museum in Tulsa, Oklahoma. These pages appear to have been torn from a ledger, and blue digits are preprinted in the upper right and upper left corners of the pages. The pages are numbered 1–8, 13–26, and 29–30; the other pages are missing. The titles of the poems are reproduced below, in the order they are presented in the ledger. Parenthetical numbers to the right of the titles indicate the ledger pages on which they appear. See the chronologically organized entries in this edition for the text of these ledger poems and for any discussion of their differences from alternate versions.

Tulledega (1)
Twilight [Eventide] (1)
Red Man's Pledge of Peace [ledger version] (2)
A Fable (2)
Happy Times for Me an' Sal (3)
Contact [part of "Chinkings"] (4)
True Friends [part of "Chinkings"] (4)
Briefly [part of "Chinkings"] (4)
The Man-Catcher (4)
Say Something (4)
Pedantry (5)
A Thin Quilt's Warmth (5)
The Boston Mountains (5)
September (5)
By the Shore of Life (5)
In Tulledega (6)

Cuba Libre (6)
Daisy (7)
Lines to Hall (8)
The Two Clouds (8)
[Fragment of "Verses Written at the Grave of McIntosh"] (13)
Autumn (13)
By the River's Brink (13)
To Our Baby, Laughing [To Baby Yahola] (14)
To the Summer Cloud (14)
A Glimpse (14)
Sea Shells (15)
When Molly Blows the Dinner-Horn (15)
Goodness [part of "Epigrams"] (15)
What Profit (16)
September (16)
To a Humming bird (16)
To a Common Flower (16)
Earth's Lilies and God's (16)
To Jim Parkinson (17)
June [Midsummer] (17)
To Hall (18)
On Piney (19)
Not Love Always (19)
Miser (19)
Be Fair [part of "Epigrams"] (20)
Sunset (20)
My Fancy [Fancy] (20)
The Milky Way (20)
The Open Sky (20)
[What sea-maid's longings dwell] [To a Sea Shell] (21)
God and the Flying Squirrel (A Creek Legend) (21)
Sunset (21)

Tender Memories [part of "Memories (Inscribed to my poet friend
   George Riley Hall)"] (22)
Mother and Baby (22)
A Common Failing (22)
The Inexpressible Thought (22)
July (23)
The Conquerors (23)
Our Deeds [A Simile] (24)
In Vain (24)
The Rattler (24)
Narcissus—A Sonnet (25)
To a Face Above the Surf (25)
Thoughts (26)
The Coyote (26)
Meaningless (26)
To a Winter Songster (29)
Trysting [Then and Now] (29–30)
A Vision (30)

Bibliography

Manuscripts and Archival Materials

American Native Press Archives, University of Arkansas at Little Rock
    Daniel F. Littlefield Jr. Collection
Bacone College, Muskogee, Oklahoma
    Alexander L. Posey's Personal Library
Bowdoin College Library, Brunswick, Maine
    George J. Mitchell Department of Special Collections and Archives
Gilcrease Museum, Tulsa, Oklahoma
    Alexander L. Posey Collection
Oklahoma Historical Society, Archives and Manuscripts Division, Oklahoma City
    Alexander L. Posey Collection
    Photo Collection
Oklahoma Historical Society Library
    Newspaper Archives
Western History Collection, University of Oklahoma, Norman
    Edward Everett Dale Collection

Secondary Sources and Suggested Reading

Chaudhuri, Jean and Joyotpaul. *A Sacred Path: The Way of the Muscogee Creeks*. Los Angeles: UCLA American Indian Studies Center, 2001.

Connelley, William Elsey. "Memoir." in *Poems of Alexander Lawrence Posey*. Comp. Minnie H. Posey. Topkea KS: Crane and Company, 1910.

Debo, Angie. *The Road to Disappearance: A History of the Creek Indians*. Norman: University of Oklahoma Press, 1941.

Lewis, David, Jr. and Ann T. Jordan. *Creek Indian Medicine Ways: The Enduring Power of Mvskoke Religion*. Albuquerque: University of New Mexico Press, 2002.

Littlefield, Daniel F., Jr. *Alex Posey: Creek Poet, Journalist, and Humorist*. Lincoln: University of Nebraska Press, 1992.

Littlefield, Daniel F., Jr., and Carol A. Petty Hunter. Introduction. *The Fus Fixico Letters*. Ed. Daniel F. Littlefield Jr. and Carol A. Petty Hunter. Lincoln: University of Nebraska Press, 1993. 1–48.

Loughridge, R. M. and David M. Hodge, *English and Muskokee Dictionary.* Okmulgee: Baptist Home Mission Board Oklahoma, [1964].

Martin, Jack B. and Margaret McKane Mauldin. *A Dictionary of Creek/Muskogee.* Lincoln: University of Nebraska Press, 2000.

Posey, Alexander. *Chinnubbie and the Owl: Muscogee (Creek) Stories, Orations, and Oral Traditions.* Ed. Matthew Wynn Sivils. Lincoln: University of Nebraska Press, 2005.

———. *The Fus Fixico Letters.* Ed. Daniel F. Littlefield Jr. and Carol A. Petty Hunter. Lincoln: University of Nebraska Press, 1993.

———. *Poems of Alexander Lawrence Posey.* Comp. Minnie H. Posey. Topeka KS: Crane and Company, 1910.

Womack, Craig S. *Red on Red: Native American Literary Separatism.* Minneapolis: University of Minnesota Press, 1999.

Wright, J. Leitch. *Creeks and Seminoles: Destruction and Regeneration of the Muscogulge People.* Lincoln: University of Nebraska Press, 1990.